The
Character
of the Poet

Poets on Poetry   Donald Hall, General Editor

The Character of the Poet

LOUIS SIMPSON

Ann Arbor

The University of Michigan Press

Copyright © by The University of Michigan 1986
All rights reserved
Published in the United States of America by
The University of Michigan Press and simultaneously
in Rexdale, Canada, by John Wiley & Sons Canada, Limited
Manufactured in the United States of America

1989   1988   1987   1986   4   3   2   1

Library of Congress Cataloging in Publication Data

Simpson, Louis Aston Marantz, 1923–
   The character of the poet.

   (Poets on poetry)
   1. Simpson, Louis Aston Marantz, 1923–   —Author-
ship—Addresses, essays, lectures. 2. Poetry—
Authorship—Addresses, essays, lectures. 3. Literature—
History and criticism—Addresses, essays, lectures.
I. Title. II. Series.
PS3537.I75C43   1986   809.1   85-31821
ISBN 0-472-09369-X
ISBN 0-472-06369-3 (pbk.)

Acknowledgments

The author wishes to thank the publishers who have given their permission to reprint these essays, poems, talks, reviews, and interviews. In each instance the publisher is identified on the essay's opening page, together with such information about the circumstances of publication as might be of interest to the reader.

Contents

I

The Character of the Poet

The Character of the Poet

For twenty years American poets have not discussed the nature of poetry. There has not been the exchange of ideas there used to be. The polemics of the Beat, the Black Mountain, the Sixties Poets, and the New York Poets are a thing of the past. The resistance to the war in Vietnam brought poets of different groups together on the same platform, and since that time they have ceased to argue—perhaps because arguing over poetry seems trivial when we are living under the shadow of nuclear annihilation.

Another reason is the ascendancy of criticism. If poets do not speak for themselves others will speak for them, and when poets vacated the platform critics rushed to take their place. Those who have no great liking for poetry like to explain it. The poets have been willing to see this happen—they are workers and not given to abstract thinking. They believe that the best literary criticism and the only kind that's likely to last is a poem.

When the theory of an art is divorced from the practice it becomes absurd. And when it acquires authority it can do considerable harm. The young people who we hope will read our poems are likely to attend a university, and there they will be exposed to the teachings of fashionable schools of crit-

---

This was a talk I gave at the University of Alabama, Tuscaloosa, on October 18, 1984. I was taking part in a symposium of poets and critics on the theme, "What Is a Poet?"

icism. Suppose such a young person were to read this poem by Wordsworth:

> A slumber did my spirit seal;
> I had no human fears:
> She seemed a thing that could not feel
> The touch of earthly years.
>
> No motion has she now, no force;
> She neither hears nor sees;
> Rolled round in earth's diurnal course,
> With rocks, and stones, and trees.

Here is the kind of explanation the young reader might be given. "'A Slumber Did My Spirit Seal' . . . enacts one version of a constantly repeated Occidental drama of the lost sun. Lucy's name of course means light. To possess her would be a means of rejoining the lost light, the father sun as *logos,* as head power and fount of meaning. . . . The death of Lucy is the loss of the *logos,* leaving the poet and his words groundless."[1]

This is not a parody but the work of a respected literary critic. His interpretation does not take into account the effect of the poem upon the reader, the poem as drama, a thing experienced. That is to say, his interpretation has nothing to do with poetry. The reflection, however, would not deter the kind of critic who reads poetry in this way. On the contrary, as such critics are not slow to admit, they think that interpretations are more important than poems.

The poet works to create an image, rhythm, and sound that will carry his thought to the heart and mind of the reader. The critic interposes to say that there is no such thing as meaning. Writing is a series of verbal signs. In writing we resort to key metaphors, and "such metaphors are self-conflicting . . . any attempt to explicate one of them proliferates into further metaphors without the possibility of coming to a halt in a literal, or 'proper' meaning."[2]

You will recall these lines by Yeats:

What shall I do with this absurdity—
O heart, O troubled heart—this caricature,
Decrepit age that has been tied to me
As to a dog's tail.

Imagine, if you can, telling Yeats that these words have no literal or proper meaning, that they are merely metaphorical. But this is what such scholars teach and, as Robert Burns said,

A set o' dull conceited hashes
Confuse their brains in college classes!

In the face of such misleading it is necessary, as perhaps never before, for poets to reaffirm the primacy of feeling, to say that poetry is not a game played with words, that it is in earnest. At the end of every idea lies a life . . . someone has paid for it. There is an end to metaphor, an angel in the gate with a fiery sword who says, "Thus far and no farther." The meanings in poems were written in blood—damn their misreadings!

We need to speak again about common life, that life people in universities appear to have put behind them. As poets this is our concern—as William Carlos Williams said, "The first thing that stands eternally in the way of really good writing is always one: the virtual impossibility of lifting to the imagination those things which lie under the direct scrutiny of the senses."

Can we make poetry out of such things? Can we write about offices and the people who work in them? About factories and the people who live in mean streets? Can we write about those large tracts between cities that are lined with houses, where so many people live? If we cannot bring these into poetry then something is missing—the life most people know.

Poets have come to think that they are different from the common man and woman, and to think that because the common man and woman does not read poetry, poetry can exclude the common man and woman. This is the fallacy that has made so much poetry in our time empty and unimpor-

· poets & non - poets

tant. Suppose Chaucer had said to himself, "The ordinary man doesn't care for poetry, so I won't write about him." This is how many poets think—consequently they write of matters that are of no concern.

How can we lift to the imagination those things which lie under the direct scrutiny of the senses? By lifting ourselves—there is no other way. We know what the poet does—she absorbs what she sees and transforms it. Whitman has described the process of absorbing:

> There was a child went forth every day,
> And the first object he look'd upon, that object he became.

But this does not explain the transforming. The poet has to be the kind of person who transforms what she sees and hears into poetry. To make the character that changes what it touches into poetry—writing poetry requires no less.

Yeats was right, there is no singing school. But I think that if we look into the lives of poets we shall find there was a time of withdrawal from the world, of silence and meditation. We tend to think of poetry as making something out of nothing, as having original ideas and fetching images from afar. But does poetry have no power in itself? No reality? What would happen if instead of trying to write poetry one allowed silence to speak?

Dante has told us how he became a poet. For nine years love had ruled his soul—the image of Beatrice was always present in his mind. Then one day he saw her walking in the street between two older women of distinguished bearing. She greeted him—he experienced the height of bliss and his senses reeled.[3]

He returned to his lonely room where, thinking of Beatrice, he fell asleep and had a vision of a lordly figure, "frightening to behold," says the poet, "yet in himself, it seemed to me, he was filled with a marvellous joy." The figure said many things of which he understood only a few, among them the words, "Ego dominus tuus," "I am your master." The figure held Beatrice in his arms; she was asleep, naked, wrapped in a crimson cloth. In one hand he held a fiery object, and he seemed to say, "Vide cor tuum," "Behold your heart." It seemed that he wakened the sleeping Beatrice and prevailed upon her to eat the glowing object in his hand. Reluctantly and hesitantly she did so. A few moments later his happiness turned to bitter grief and, weeping, he gathered Beatrice in his arms and together they seemed to ascend into the heavens.

The poet felt such anguish at their departure that he woke. It was, he tells us, the first of the last nine hours of the night. Pondering what he had seen in his dream, he decided to make it known to a number of poets who were famous at the time. "As I had already tried my hand at composing in rhyme, I decided to write a sonnet in which I would greet all Love's faithful servants; and so, requesting them to interpret my dream, I described what I had seen. This was the sonnet beginning, 'To every captive soul.'"

With the passing of the old religious world poets no longer thought of themselves as inspired by a god, but still they felt prompted to write by a power outside themselves. For Wordsworth this power spoke through nature. He tells how he first became aware that he was to be a poet. He was returning home at dawn from a night spent in "dancing, gaiety, and mirth," with "slight shocks of young love-liking interspersed," when

> Magnificent
> The morning rose, in memorable pomp,
> Glorious as e'er I had beheld—in front,
> The sea lay laughing at a distance; near,
> The solid mountains shone...[4]

The scene before him included laborers going out to till the fields. "Ah! need I say, dear Friend," he says, addressing Coleridge,

> that to the brim
> My heart was full; I made no vows, but vows
> Were then made for me; bond unknown to me

Was given, that I should be, else sinning greatly,
A dedicated Spirit. On I walked
In thankful blessedness, which yet survives.

I believe that all true poets feel a sense of dedication, and that this comes to them in solitude and silence. The silence of which Pascal spoke, the silence of infinite spaces, is terrifying, and most avoid it, but poetry feeds on silence. To apprehend the silence of the universe is to wish to break it, to speak to those who are in the same boat with ourselves.

The measure of a man, said Ortega, is the amount of solitude he can stand, and great poets are those who have listened greatly. Rilke speaks of this.

Voices. Voices. Listen, my heart, as only
saints have listened: until the gigantic call lifted them
off the ground; yet they kept on, impossibly,
kneeling and didn't notice at all:
so complete was their listening. Not that you could endure
God's voice—far from it. But listen to the voice of the wind
and the ceaseless message that forms itself out of silence.[5]

The task of the poet is to put into words the message that formed itself out of silence.

"What is a poet?" Wordsworth asks, and answers the question himself: "He is a man speaking to men [he might have said a man or woman speaking to men and women] . . . a man, it is true, endowed with more lively sensibility, more enthusiasm and tenderness, who has a greater knowledge of human nature, and a more comprehensive soul, than are supposed to be common among mankind: a man pleased with his own passions and volitions, and who rejoices more than other men in the spirit of life that is in him; delighting to contemplate similar volitions and passions as manifested in the goings-on of the Universe, and habitually impelled to create them where he does not find them."[6]

Amen to that! I am pleased by the pleasure Wordsworth takes in his own passions and volitions. It is good to have him come right out and say so. I also like the sentence about feeling impelled to create them where he does not find them.

The idea of the poet as having a greater knowledge of human nature than the ordinary person, and a vitality he wishes to impart, has dwindled since Wordsworth wrote. The poet's conviction that he has something important to say, some god- or wind-given message, has almost disappeared. Must we then talk only of ourselves and be reduced to writing confessions? In recent years it has seemed so—the poet as alienated man or woman, this has been the subject of much contemporary verse. I need hardly point out how uninteresting the subject finally is. It has dwindled into this kind of writing.

> Most of us, though white,
> Belonged to no country clubs
> And had perfectly reasonable ideas.
> I drove my parents' third car, the Toyota . . .[7]

In poetry-writing workshops all over the country writers, having been told that they must describe things accurately and be sincere—and if you asked them who said so, they might say Williams—are writing these dreary little exercises in futility.

> I learned to write ninety words a minute.
> I quit the band because I wasn't stupid.
> At concerts no one sat with me;
> They called me bad names and didn't like me.

The idea behind such writing is that if you are sincere it will be poetry. But it isn't—it doesn't lift anything to the imagination. One could, in fact, expatiate on the positive dislike of imagination that lies behind such writing—it is the form Puritanism takes in our time. The obsession with one's personal history, one's body, one's parents—American poetry has been going round and round the self like a squirrel in a cage. There is no way to break out except by regaining the idea of poetry as a force, a reality. I am not saying that poetry should not speak with feeling—I have said that it must—but confessional writing is a dead end. If poetry is to be important it must regain Dante's and Wordsworth's sense of the importance of what they were saying. Poetry must be conceived as a force beyond the self, and the poet as the medium of this force.

I do not see how this can be felt unless one has the vision of a community. For a long time I tried to describe the essential quality of a poet, that which makes the poet different from the mere writer of verse, some vibrancy of emotion in his language. I have come to think that this proceeds from his sense of being a part in the scheme of things, and from this only. All other matters having to do with poetry are secondary to this. There is no word or phrase to describe this quality in a poet. We speak of the poet's style or voice—we may examine his choice of words and use of syntax. But from what does the voice proceed? From his sense that his thoughts count for something with his fellow human beings, that they are helping to build a community.

The poets we call great express such a sense through their works. It is true of Dante, Wordsworth, Akhmatova . . . any memorable poet you can name. When we read them we feel not only, as Whitman said, that we are touching flesh and blood, but that the life in the words is far-reaching and significant. That the poets felt this themselves there can be no doubt—it was the ground of their proceeding. Wordsworth, in the lines I have quoted, knew that he had been dedicated to carry out a task and that if he refused he would be "sinning greatly." In *The Prelude* he says that the love of nature leads to the love of man. Similar passages are to be found in the lives of all poets whose words have power to move us.

One does not live to oneself, and in order to write poetry one must believe in something. The old gods are dead or sleeping, and the nineteenth-century ideal of Beauty expressed through Art is of no comfort to twentieth-century men and women who face the prospect of the destruction of everything in some nuclear holocaust. What then can the poet hope for? A community of hearts and minds that will extend across nations and leap the barriers erected by governments. Poets may represent the millions who have no voice of their own. Poets may speak to other poets and through them to all who are filled with the same hopes and fears. Through poetry there may be an exchange of the best thoughts of people around the world. If this is called visionary I would like to know what practical alternative is proposed? What else can poets believe if they do not believe in this?

Am I asking for poets to be political? In the largest and deepest sense, yes. I am asking for poetry that represents the lives we really have and makes our thoughts and feelings known. I am not asking for propaganda. Poets are free men and women—they cannot serve an ideology, for to do so is not to be free.

Are you a poet? Is your thinking real? Does it touch hearts and minds? If so, your writing is political.

There may still be some who think that I am asking for some crude, propagandistic kind of writing. Then let me read a passage from a writer I admire greatly, Joseph Conrad. He is a novelist, but no matter—on this point the concerns of the poet and the writer of prose are the same. Many are familiar with Conrad's statement of his method: "My task which I am trying to achieve is, by the power of the written word to make you hear, to make you feel—it is before all, to make you see."[8] What many readers have not noticed is the larger statement that follows:

> To snatch in a moment of courage, from the remorseless rush of time, a passing phase of life, is only the beginning of the task. The task approached in tenderness and faith is to hold up unquestioningly, without choice and without fear, the rescued fragment before all eyes in the light of a sincere mood. It is to show its vibration, its colour, its form; and through its move- ment, its form, and its colour, reveal the substance of its truth—disclose its inspiring secret: the stress and passion with- in the core of each convincing moment. In a single-minded attempt of that kind, if one be deserving and fortunate, one may perchance attain to such clearness of sincerity that at last the presented vision of regret or pity, of terror or mirth, shall

awake in the hearts of the beholders that feeling of unavoidable solidarity in mysterious origin, in toil, in uncertain fate, which binds men to each other and all mankind to the visible world.

Thus the author of *The Shadow Line* . . . With such a sense of purpose a poet could go far. Though imagination may not reach to another world as it did centuries ago, still, the common road leads somewhere.

For a hundred years lyric poetry has been placed on a pedestal. Can it be only coincidence that this has been accompanied by a general decline of interest in poetry? It is the nature of the lyric to express a subjective mood and ignore the outer reality. It is to be expected that such writing will interest very few.

The separation of the lyric from narrative and discursive writing began with Poe and was adopted by the Symbolists as an absolute principle. Mallarmé wished to reduce to a minimum all elements but the lyric, so as to arrive at "pure poetry." He placed narrative and discursive poetry in an inferior category. A critic has described the reason behind this kind of thinking as "a revulsion from crass reality and an ardent inspiration towards a finer life. The poet," says this critic, "denounces with searing scorn the revolting happiness of those gross appetites that are so easily satisfied."[9] Among the gross appetites, however, Mallarmé did not include his own for tobacco.

> All the soul summarized
> when slowly we exhale
> smoke-rings that arise
> and other rings annul
>
> attests some cigar . . .[10]

The ash of Mallarmé's cigar was not pure. Words do have meanings, unavoidably, and "pure poetry" is no purer than the other kind, it is only less substantial. If the Symbolists had carried to the logical conclusion their program for poetry that would approach "the condition of music," they would have given up writing. For why have words when one can have music itself?

The wish for "pure poetry" has brought about writing that is as far from meaning as one can get without lapsing into nonsense, and frequently it crosses the line. Here is a passage from Wallace Stevens's "Notes Toward a Supreme Fiction":

> The romantic intoning, the declaimed clairvoyance
> Are parts of apotheosis, appropriate
> And of its nature, the idiom thereof.
>
> They differ from reason's click-clack, its applied
> Enflashings. But apotheosis is not
> The origin of the major man. He comes,
>
> Compact in invincible foils, from reason,
> Lighted at midnight by the studious eye,
> Swaddled in revery, the object of
>
> The hum of thoughts evaded in the mind,
> Hidden from other thoughts, he that reposes
> On a breast forever precious to the touch . . .

This sounds like a man philosophizing, and if one studies the passage one can make sense of it. But this writing is either sound and no sense, or sense without sound, for in disassembling the phrases to find what they mean, one loses their effect as sound. The later poetry of Wallace Stevens is a case of the disassociation of sensibility Eliot pointed to years ago as a defect of Milton's verse and besetting defect of Victorian verse. Stevens's poetry is not philosophy and his philosophy is not poetry.

With us, however, the wish to be pure has not expressed itself as music—more commonly it has led to imagistic writing, poems that consist only of images.

If poetry is to matter we must put in our poems those elements that have been excluded as impure. This means breaking with the standards set by the academy, by those who have made emptiness a virtue—who have elevated Stevens above Frost, above Williams and Pound and Eliot; who have praised to the skies James Merrill's musings over a Ouija board, and have told us that Amy Clampitt is a poet.

I came across the following lines in the *New Yorker*. The subject is some pigeons that keep returning to perch on a building that no longer exists—it has been knocked down. The pigeons are described as

> descending yet again the roofless
> staircase of outmoded custom, the
> soon-to-be-obliterated stations
> of nostalgia—as though the air
> itself might wince at the stigmata
> of the dispossessed, the razed,
> the *triste,* the unaccounted for.[11]

The pigeons are said to be descending as though the air might wince. This is perfect nonsense. Then consider the word *stigmata,* the offensiveness of using it in this connection. C. H. Sisson, writing about Herbert Read, says that "it is as if the facility of Read's discursive mind was such that the barriers to expression, the sense of which is often a preliminary to poetry, did not exist."[12] The same might be said of Amy Clampitt: her mind, facile and discursive, encounters no barriers. And where are the stigmata located? On the wings of the pigeons? Their feet and sides? Are the stigmata to be seen on the building that is no longer there? The word *razed* in the phrase, "The stigmata / of the dispossessed, the razed," indicates that there are stigmata on a nonexistent building. The word *triste* adds the final touch of silly affectation.

This is what comes of straining to be poetic. But poetry is not something one has to invent—it is there in the object, waiting to be seen. As Pound said, "The natural object is always the adequate symbol." Williams said it also: "No ideas but in things."

The similarities between objects, that is, metaphors, don't have to be invented—they are there if you look for them. And the more they rise of their own accord, the more striking they will be, affecting the reader with the power of a natural force.

No sooner does an American set up as a poet than he begins to suffer from what a friend of Whitman's called the "beauty disease." He thinks that poetry has to be written in a special language and that subjects have to be farfetched. This brings on the inanity of which I have given examples, a kind of anorexia nervosa, so that poetry becomes thin to the point of disappearing. There is no cure but immersion in the common life and the language, as Wordsworth said, really used by men.

Common life since the Industrial Revolution has been increasingly antipoetic. Baudelaire found a sordid enchantment in the city, comparing it to an ant-heap that at dusk disgorged prostitutes, crooks, and thieves. Whitman found a grandeur in the streets of Brooklyn and Manhattan:

> Burn high your fires, foundry chimneys! cast black
> shadows at nightfall! cast red and yellow light over the
> tops of the houses!

In our time the poetry of cities has become more elusive—how is one to find poetry in an office where secretaries sit typing or the aisle of a supermarket? Yet it is imperative for poetry to deal with such material—it is all around us. Not only urban scenes but the minds of the people need to be represented, and I don't mean some programmatic literature about the working man or woman such as Socialist Realism produced—I mean poetry about the people you actually meet and the ideas they have, including the banal, foolish ones.

This is the step that has to be taken, and some poets have already taken it, though you won't find them in the *New Yorker*. The following poem by Toi Derricotte is titled "Fears of the Eighth Grade."

> when i ask what things they fear,
> their arms raise like soldiers volunteering for battle:
> fear to go into a dark room, my murderer is waiting;
> fear of taking a shower, someone will stab me;
> fear of being kidnapped, raped;
> fear of dying in war.

when i ask how many fear this,
all the children raise their hands.

i think of this little box of consecrated land,
the bombs somewhere else,
the dead children in their mothers' arms,
women crying at the gates of the palace.

how thin the veneer!
the paper towels, napkins, toilet paper—everything
burned up in a day.

these children see the city after armageddon;
the demons stand visible in the air
between their friends talking;
they see fire in a spring day
the instant before conflagration:
they feel blood through closed faucets
& touch sharks crawling at the bottom of the sea.

imagination & transformation

Yes, the poet "has a greater knowledge of human nature,
and a more comprehensive soul, than are supposed to be
common among mankind." She has lifted herself, and so she
is able to carry things with her into thought, transform experience into significant thought.

The city is antipoetic, the suburbs are antipoetic, but turn
to the people and subjects for poetry abound. This is the
solution to our present difficulty, the emptiness and unimpor-
tance of American verse. We need a poetry of human situations. Imagination does not consist in thinking of surrealist
imagery—one could write like that forever, as Dr. Johnson
remarked, if one abandoned one's mind to it. Imagination
shows us the possibilities in human nature—it says, like the
dwarf in the tale by Grimm, "Something human is dearer to
me than the wealth of all the world."

There is a poem by Thomas Hardy, "Neutral Tones," that
presents a scene: a pond, a white sun, gray leaves scattered
under a tree. This is the setting for a meeting between a man
and woman who have been lovers and are no longer so. They
are having a sad, bitter discussion about, as Hardy puts it,
"Which lost the more by our love."

16

> The smile on your mouth was the deadest thing
> Alive enough to have strength to die;
> And a grin of bitterness swept thereby
>   Like an ominous bird a-wing . . .

The remarkable thing is the amount of passion Hardy gets into his neutral tones, the amount of volition. He bleaches all color out of the scene to go with the bleaching out of love. Then, as if to show what poetry can do, he injects the scene with his own interest, fixes in memory the "God-curst" sun, tree, and pond edged with grayish leaves. The scene has become emblematic—it might be hung as a picture to illustrate the ending of love and the tears of things.

Hardy certainly seems to have been impelled to create volitions and passions where he did not find them. At the passage of this small man things were charged with energy and assumed a significance. As he says, he was a man who used to notice such things, and in return they have noticed him. The slightest poem of Hardy's vibrates with the life that was in him.

One must have that kind of energy, that interest. One must have a theme. It is the theme in a narrative by Hardy that makes it live as the narrative poems of other Victorians do not. Hardy's character as a poet is expressed in his theme—he has chosen to tell this story and no other out of some inner necessity. The necessity returns in poem after poem—it has to do with the gaining and losing of love between men and women. The theme is of vital concern to Hardy—it animates not only his characters but their surroundings.

Robert Frost, referring to some contemporary poets, said that they were not much troubled by anything that was in them. And Yeats has a speaker in a poem say, "What, be a singer born and lack a theme?" It is the theme that gives poetry its authenticity. I have spoken of the poet's training in solitude and silence. What he discovers there, the messages the wind delivers to him, are the themes of his writing. He emerges from solitude as the Indian woke from the dream that gave him a name and a place in the tribe.

— not personal

The art of poetry consists in discovering the themes that are proper to oneself. There can be no formulas for such discoveries. Keats said that the world was a vale of soul-making. For the poet it is the vale where he makes his theme. The poet's theme is his true self.

It is to be differentiated from the merely personal life, as the Indian's big dream was different from little dreams. In our time there has been an appetite for biographies of poets, but with a few exceptions—the life of Keats by Gittings, of Johnson by Bate—they are beside the point. Proust said it once and for all:

> By failing to see the gulf that separates the writer from the man of the world, by failing to understand that the writer's true self is manifested in his books alone, and that what he shows to men of the world . . . is merely a man of the world like themselves, Sainte-Beuve came to set up that celebrated Method which, according to Taine, Bourget, and the rest of them, is his title to fame, and which consists, if you would understand a poet or writer, in greedily catechising those who knew him, who saw quite a lot of him, who can tell us how he conducted himself in regard to women, etc.—precisely, that is, at every point where the poet's true self is not involved.

The method Proust describes, is that not exactly the way biographers have gone about describing the lives of our poets—how one has written the life of Delmore Schwartz, another the life of Robert Lowell, and another the life of John Berryman? What did one learn from these books? That the men suffered from vanity, from drink, from mental illness. What did one learn about the nature of poetry? Practically nothing.

The theme is the man. "You want," says Conrad's storyteller, "a deliberate belief"—another way of describing the writer's theme. Conrad distinguishes this from principles, by which he seems to mean morality. "Principles won't do. Acquisitions, pretty rags—rags that would fly off at the first good shake."[13]

The poet may be helped to discover his true self or theme by looking at pictures and statues and reading books—what Yeats calls "monuments of unageing intellect," though they need not be so monumental—Yeats himself read Madame Blavatsky. The book that nourishes one's theme may as well be some simple book read in childhood as Dante or the Book of Job.

The poet can only speak of his theme, that which is proper to him. The mere writer of verse can speak of anything with equanimity. "A rhymer, and a *poet,* are two things."

"With talent," said Ingres, "you do what you like. With genius, you do what you can."

Those who have followed me so far may wonder why, feeling as I do about a "poetry of situations," I have not spoken about prose fiction rather than verse. There is a great difference between verse and prose, and I would not give up the one thing verse has in its favor: an absolute form. We do not know why certain people who are called poets feel compelled to write in lines—this is a great mystery. If the poet were a dancer she would dance; a musician, she would compose music; but she is a poet and so she writes . . . in lines. Lines are the form of her soul. The movement of the poem corresponds to a movement of the poet's soul.

There is something demonic about the writing of poetry, some power the poet wishes to exact over the reader's emotions. The rhythm and breaking of the line determine that the reader shall respond in a certain way and no other. Measure compels. It is different with prose—the reader is allowed to get loose of the writer's emotion and drift into revery.

Writing in lines appears to establish an absolute order of language—though of course it only appears to do so. It is the poet's task to make us feel that the order is absolute, but any poet who has done thirty or forty drafts of a poem knows the uncertainty of such things. We aim at perfection knowing that we can never hit it. We do not finish, we leave off.

Not only does the line compel, every syllable does. As Coleridge said, poetry proposes to itself "such delight from the *whole*, as is compatible with a distinct gratification from each component part."[14] We take pleasure in each syllable, word, and phrase as it occurs. There is a pleasure in fine sentences too, the prose of Flaubert, but as a rule prose does not give the effect of an absolute order of language.

Now that I have brought my subject down to the actual writing I would like to step back and speak once more of poetry as an act of communion. "The Poet," says Wordsworth, "binds together by passion and knowledge the vast empire of human society, as it is spread over the whole earth, over all time."

There are those who would reject this idea. W. H. Auden was such a one—poetry, he said emphatically, does nothing, it is a purely gratuitous activity. Others who might admit that poetry can change the individual would deny that it can bring a community into being. Statements such as Wordsworth's, and the longer statement by Conrad I quoted earlier, they would say are orective and conative in nature—"orective because [the authors'] view of the ultimate function of literature is a matter of what is desired rather than what they thought to be a fact; conative because they are really talking about the creative direction which they themselves are trying to take as writers."[15]

Solidarity, then, is only an idea. But so was the republic we live under, and a dozen actions we perform every day originated with an idea. I have never understood the kind of person who, dressed in a suit that came from an idea in the mind of a tailor, and having dined on a meal that was an idea in the mind of a cook, will talk scornfully of ideas and idealism.

The physicist has a theory about the atom without the supporting facts. He proceeds on the assumption that his theory is true, and lo, the suspected particle swims into our ken, where he said it would be. It is the same with poetry. The poet believes that people will sympathize with her ideas, and this enables her to write with an emotion that moves them to sympathize. The poet's faith then stands on accomplished fact—she has created passions and volitions where she did not find them. If poets are the liars Plato said they are, poems are not—they become part of our thinking and we see the world by the light of poetry.

If it be said that binding hearts and minds is only an idea, a feeling we have when we are reading poems or hearing them, far from this being an argument against the social effectiveness of poetry, it is a powerful argument in its favor. If it is in poetry, and only there, that human sympathy is found, such writing must have a unique, irreplaceable value. It is not the expression of a faith but the community we are seeking, the thing itself.

NOTES

1. Hillis Miller, in M. H. Abrams and James Ackerman, *Theories of Criticism: Essays in Literature and Art* (Washington, D.C.: Library of Congress, 1984), 28.

2. Miller, 22–23.

3. Dante Alighieri, *La Vita Nuova,* trans. Barbara Reynolds (Middlesex, U.K.: Penguin Books, 1969), 31–32.

4. William Wordsworth, *The Prelude,* Book Fourth.

5. *The Collected Poetry of Rainer Maria Rilke,* ed. and trans. Stephen Mitchell (New York: Random House, 1982), 153.

6. Preface to "Lyrical Ballads," 1800.

7. Laurie Henry, "Downtown Newberry Destroyed by Tornado," the *American Poetry Review* 13 (May/June 1984): 48.

8. Preface to *The Nigger of the 'Narcissus.'*

9. Lloyd James Austin, "Presence and Poetry of Stéphane Mallarmé: International Reputation and Intellectual Impact," 1973. In *The Symbolist Movement in the Literature of European Languages,* ed. Anna Balakian (Budapest: Akadémiai Kiadó, 1982), 45.

10. Stéphane Mallarmé, "Autres Poëmes et Sonnets," *Selected Poems,* trans. C. F. MacIntyre (Berkeley: University of California Press, 1957), 101.

11. Amy Clampitt, "Vacant Lot with Tumbleweed and Pigeons," the *New Yorker,* January 30, 1984, 32.

12. *English Poetry 1900–1950: An Assessment* (Manchester, U.K.: Carcanet New Press, 1981), 186.

13. "Heart of Darkness."

14. Samuel Taylor Coleridge, *Biographia Literaria,* Chapter 14.

15. Ian Watt, *Conrad in the Nineteenth Century* (Berkeley: University of California Press, 1979), 80–81.

auto-biography

My Beginnings

"Come back to the ways things used to be," says the TV commercial. "Make it Jamaica. Again!" I have mixed feelings about this. I am the other Jamaican, a child of the middle class, some of us white, some "colored," but all of us borrowing our manners and prejudices from the English. We had servants, and tea was served every afternoon on the veranda at four o'clock. After the Second World War, Jamaica was made independent of Britain. I am sure Jamaicans don't want things to be the way they used to be.

My father, Aston, was a native. His family went back to Scotland, and there was a Frenchman mixed up in it somewhere. Aston was a lawyer, and he had an older brother, also a lawyer, who had been mayor of Kingston. During the earthquake of 1907 Uncle Bertie lost a leg and was known thereafter as Corkfoot. At election time the calypso singers had a song about him:

> Corkfoot Simpson yuh vagabon'
> an if ah ketch yuh ah chop off de odder one.

My mother was born in Russia. She came to New York with her family when she was a young girl and went to work in the

This essay first appeared in the *New York Times Book Review,* March 14, 1982, under the title, "The Sound of Words for Their Own Sake." This was misleading: the phrase, taken out of context, gave the impression that I care only for the sound of words, which is at variance with my thought and practice. Copyright © 1982 by The New York Times Company. Reprinted by permission.

garment district. Then she became an actress, in silent movies. There was an opening for a young woman in Annette Kellerman's company of bathing beauties. My mother tried out for the part. The test was to jump into a tank full of water and act as though she were drowning. She jumped and gave a convincing performance, for she couldn't swim a stroke, and when they pulled her out she was hired.

The bathing beauties came to Jamaica to make a movie called *Neptune's Daughter* and stayed at the Myrtle Bank Hotel in Kingston. My father and some other unmarried men went to have a look at them. Then my mother fell out with the director. He wanted his beauties to pose in the nude. My mother and another young woman refused, and they were given their tickets back to New York. My father went there to court her, and they were married. He brought her back to Jamaica, and they set up housekeeping near Cross Roads in the middle-class style. My mother handed the tea cups around and joined the Liguanea Club, but she did not fit in. She was far too emotional.

I trace my beginnings as a writer to the stories my mother read to me—Oscar Wilde's "The Happy Prince" was one of her favorites—and the stories she told about her childhood in Russia. She spoke of Cossacks and wolves, of freezing in winter, and rats. In Volhynia rats carried the typhus bacilli that had killed her sister Lisa and almost killed her.

My love of stories became a family joke. When one of my mother's sisters came from New York to stay with us for a while, the first thing I would say was "Tell me a story." And when she had finished, "Tell me another."

I also went to the garden boy for anything I could get out of him. The garden boy clipped the hedges and watered the flowers. He rolled the tennis court, and when there were lawn-tennis parties he ran about and returned the balls. When my father went bird shooting, the garden boy went along to retrieve the birds. When my father obtained a motor launch and took us out in the harbor on Sundays, the garden boy served as an able seaman.

I speak of a garden boy, but there were several. They came and went, dismissed for some infraction of the rules. I tested them all to find if they had any stories. It was Nancy stories I was after, tales of Bro'er Nancy—the Daddy Long Legs spider—Bro'er Alligator, Bro'er Tiger, Bro'er Donkey, and Bro'er Crow. Some of the stories were frightening. There was one in which Bro'er Alligator's house had a roof made of bones. But Wordsworth tells us that imagination is fostered by fear as well as beauty.

Beautiful the island surely was—the most beautiful island in the world, said H. M. Tomlinson. I remember sunsets viewed from the mountain where I went to school. There was a plain stretching below, and beyond it an empty sea. The plain was arid and as empty as the sea. Over to the west, as night fell, lights began to shine from the settlement at the mouth of Black River.

We were taught by Englishmen. In all our subjects except science and mathematics we were required to write essays. There was English composition, of course, but we also wrote essays on history, geography, and Scripture. We translated Latin and French into English sentences. I entered Munro College when I was nine, and eight years later, when I left, I could write on any subject with facility. On one of my report cards, however, the headmaster remarked that I was in danger of becoming too facile—the results were better when I took the time to think. I have heeded the warning: I write sentences over and over, and a poem may go through fifty drafts.

Outside the classroom I read historical novels by G. A. Henty and Erckmann-Chatrian, farcical novels by W. W. Jacobs and P. G. Wodehouse, and novels of romance and adventure. Every Christmas my father gave me the big red *Chums* annual, which was full of stories for boys. There would be a serial about English schoolboys, the kind we were supposed to be. The hero and his friends were manly and straightforward and not too clever, the sort England could depend on. There was a fat boy who was always eating pies and jam and being caned, whereupon he would howl with pain. Great fun! There was an aristocratic boy with a monocle who said, "Bai Jove!", a dusky boy from India who spoke babu English but was good at cricket, and a bully and his cronies who smoked cigarettes and, you could surmise, had other bad habits.

When I was fourteen I wrote an essay on the coronation of George VI for a competition being held by the *Daily Gleaner*. Having read an article in the same newspaper that described the procession to Westminster Abbey, I let my imagination have free rein and painted a picture of gaily caparisoned horses, gilded coaches, and lords and ladies graciously bowing to an adoring populace. For an original touch I found fault with Shakespeare for some lines he had written saying that a king's life was not all it was cracked up to be. My essay won the first prize and was published in the *Gleaner*. With the five pounds of my prize money, a lot in those days—my weekly allowance was two shillings and sixpence, about fifty cents—I bought a bicycle and went riding all over Kingston, avoiding the tram lines, in lanes shadowed by bamboo and eucalyptus, by hedges powdered with dust. Sometimes I rode by the house where Maria Roberts lived, hoping that she would appear and admit that she was just as much in love with me as I was with her, but this never came to pass.

The next year, I won the second prize in a short-story competition, and this too was published in the *Gleaner*. I wrote about a young man who came from the country to Kingston to find work—as our garden boys did. My protagonist arrived in Kingston just in time for an earthquake. I based my description of the earthquake on the movie *San Francisco*, which had recently been playing at the Carib Theater. I had him save the life of a stranger, who thereupon rewarded him by handing over his wallet. I had not read the Horatio Alger stories but discovered the formula for a hero on my own: a willing disposition and good luck.

My hero returned to his hut in the mountains to find his mother dying. (My mother had divorced my father and gone back to the States—she came back to Jamaica from time to time to see my brother and me.) The story ended with the words, "Too late, too late!"

I had been reading Thomas Hardy. I was also reading novels by Thackeray, Dickens, Austen, and Conrad. My cousin Sybil, who worked in the public library in Kingston, tried to dissuade me from taking out a novel by Zola, but she could not actually prevent it. I read modern novels such as *Point Counterpoint* that were said to be risqué. I read D. H. Lawrence and was eyeing the copy of *Ulysses* my brother had got from England by mail order.

I was also reading poetry and trying to write it. In school we were taught Shakespeare, Shelley, and Keats, and the "Georgian poets" whom our English masters were fond of because they described English meadows and English birds and beasts. We were required to memorize poems by W. H. Davies, John Masefield, and Walter de la Mare.

I discovered A. E. Housman for myself, and for a year or two read his lyrics with the kind of sympathy that a young American now feels for rock. I lay beneath the willows that lined the driveway to the school, reading Housman's ballads about "lads" who were betrayed by "lasses" and killed a rival and were going to swing for it. Or they enlisted in the Lancers and traveled to a foreign land and found a soldier's grave.

Then I discovered the poems of T. S. Eliot. I was becoming sophisticated.

My father and Norman Manley would sometimes work together on a case. Manley had studied for the bar in England and married an English woman. In later years he would be the Prime Minister of Jamaica, and his son Michael would be Prime Minister in his turn.

Mrs. Manley was one of the extraordinary individuals England produced—along with the stuffed shirts—gifted people who broke through the barriers of their class and education. With her encouragement, a number of young people came together to discuss politics, literature, and art. We spoke of the changes that were taking place and looked forward to the day when Jamaica would be independent. As long as we were colonials we would feel, and be, inferior.

I knew very little about politics, but from my reading of the "Oxford poets," W. H. Auden, Louis MacNeice, and others, I had imbibed leftist ideas. Moreover, the successes of Hitler and Mussolini drove one to the left. But my writing remained apolitical: poems about trees, and the sea, and a poem about passengers riding in a bus. I published a short story called "In Love and Puberty" that offended my Aunt May—as I recall, she sniffed. These writings came out in a periodical called *Public Opinion.* I was becoming a name, a "writer."

My father had expected me to be a lawyer, but he had died, and it was up to me to choose. There was no question at all in my mind. I wanted to write, and I wanted to get out of Jamaica.

Why? Because I was young and wanted to see the world. It was as simple as that. There was talk of my going to Oxford, but I could only do so if I won a scholarship, and that was most uncertain. Then my mother wrote and asked if I would like to come to New York for a visit. I came and did not go back.

I entered Columbia College, and for some time continued to think of myself as a revolutionary, looking back to my connection with *Public Opinion.* I went to see *Ten Days That Shook the World* at the Stanley Theater and movies in which Joe Stalin puffed benignly on his pipe and patted little children on the head. Over in Germany, Adolf Hitler was also patting little children on the head; but that was Nazism, quite a different thing.

Then I went off to the war, three years of it. I began with the tanks and finished with the 101st Airborne Division. We fought in Normandy, Holland, Belgium, and Germany. I came back from the war much changed. To this day when I see an open field I think, How are we going to get across that?

After the war I went back to Columbia and wrote furiously. I wrote short stories, one of which was published by *Esquire,* and a novel without characters or a plot. Then I had what used to be called a "nervous breakdown"—under repeated bombardment my brains had become unhinged. All this writing prose made something snap—they were banging like a loose shutter in the wind.

After some months I came out of it. Columbia College wouldn't have me back, but the School of General Studies would. I took courses there in the evenings. I did the nightshift on the *New York Herald Tribune.* But I had no interest in reporting. I got a job in an import-export firm, packing ballpoint pens and damaged stockings for export to Europe. And I wrote poems.

To write prose you have to be stable, day in day out, and I wasn't stable yet. Besides, my ambition to be a famous writer had been dampened by my breakdown. I no longer had the confidence you need to pour out words, page after page, to create characters, to believe in your own fantasies. It appeared that I would not be a novelist.

But with poetry I could express an idea or tell a story in a brief space, and it would hang together. Besides, I loved the rhythm and the sound of words for their own sake. So I wrote poems about the war and other matters, and when I was twenty-six published my first book, at my own expense. I was living in Paris that year, and I went to a printer and paid him $500 to make 500 copies of my poems. *The Arrivistes* was priced at $2. I sent some copies out for review and gave some away, and the rest were stolen. They still turn up on the market from time to time, looking brand-new, selling for $300.

So I was going to write poems. I hadn't intended this—it was the way I could go. A matter of temperament, and the way the land lay, what I was able to do and what I could not.

From time to time I have asked myself what I hope to accomplish by writing poems. Poetry is of no importance in the United States. The people in the town where I live, who talk to me about the movies or television shows they have seen, do not read my poems. It would not occur to them to buy one of my books. Then who do I write for?

I don't write for myself—what would be the point of that? Writing is hard work—as I've said, it is mostly rewriting. On the other hand, I don't write for the "public." There are writers of verse who manage to reach a fairly wide audience, but I am not gifted that way. In order to have a public I would have to give up writing the kind of poem I like to write. There would be no pleasure in it, any more than there would be in writing for myself.

I write poems in order to express feelings I have had since I was a child. As Wordsworth says, the feelings may not be as spontaneous as they used to be, but years bring a "philosophic mind," and you can express your feelings as you could not when you were a child.

I have always felt that there is a power and intelligence in things. I felt it as a boy when I watched the sun setting from the top of a mountain and rode a bicycle in the lanes of Kingston and walked along the shore, listening to the sea. I felt that power when I first saw Manhattan rise out of the Atlantic, the towers a poet describes as "moody water-loving giants." During the war I felt there was an intelligence watching and listening. Others had expressed their sense of it. When I came upon an old trench of the First World War I remembered the lines by Wilfred Owen:

> Our brains ache, in the merciless iced east winds that knive
>   us . . .
> Wearied we keep awake because the night is silent . . .

Weeks later, in the snow around Bastogne, I could apply these words to myself and my companions. I write poems, as did men and women who lived before me, to express the drama, the terror and beauty of life.

A Response to the
Jewish Book Council
May 3, 1981

A few words about my background seem called for: I was born in Jamaica in the British West Indies of a Jewish mother and Gentile father. When I was growing up I did not know that I was a Jew, and knew nothing of Jewish life and culture. At the age of seventeen I emigrated to the United States, came to know my mother's family, and understood that I was Jewish.

At that time the Second World War had begun, and the Jews in Europe were being persecuted. Our family had a number of relatives in southern Russia. My grandmother Pearl Marantz knew these people—in the 1930s she had traveled to Russia and visited her relatives. She continued to write to them and assist them in any way she could, for they were not rich people. But now, in the early 1940s, the news that came out of Russia was ominous. When the war covered that part of the world there was silence. As one of my poems says,

> The village
> and all who dwelled therein
> have been swept from the face of the earth.

As I have said, I had no formal Jewish education, unless reading the Old Testament in English can be thought of as an

---

Caviare at the Funeral had received the Jewish Book Council award in poetry. This talk, somewhat shortened, was published in the *Jewish Book Annual* 39 (1981).

education. At the school I attended in Jamaica we were required to read the Old Testament as well as the New, and the psalms of David, translated into English, became a part of my thinking. To this day the imagery of desert and rocky places presents itself to my mind's eye as though it were my native ground. I do not need to be told how the Jews lived three thousand years ago—I understand the despair of the people in the wilderness better than I understand their lives in the suburbs. My reading of the Old Testament, before I knew that I was a Jew, gave me a love of the solitudes in which the God of the ancient tribes appeared and spoke.

I suspect that my ideas about the Jews are too much influenced by my own feeling of solitude as a child, my longing for some power that would arrive from outside, do something spectacular and awe-inspiring, and set everything right. The lives of American Jews, especially those who live comfortably, have little in common with my vision of a wilderness in which a tribe wanders, following a cloud of smoke by day and a pillar of fire by night.

During the Second World War the Jews suffered again as they had under the pharaohs, and their fate was even more terrible. But though I could imagine what the Jews in Europe suffered, this did not increase my understanding of Jewish life. The Jew who observes Jewish customs and keeps the Sabbath and the religious holidays knows far more than I about the meaning of Judaism. To wander in a desert or die in a concentration camp is not the definition of a Jew. The object of living for the Jew, as for everyone in the world, is to be happy. It is to cherish life. The Jew has suffered for his faith and therefore has been compelled to be curious about the purpose of life, to find a justifying design in experience. His happiness consists in seeing that justifying design. He believes that life is lived to some purpose, and that it is good. The Jew believes that ultimately there is a community of man and God.

My poems reflect these ideas—my feelings about being a Jew and my criticisms of society, especially where it fails to show a sense of community and purposive life. My poems are therefore an anomaly in the present literary scene. At the present time American poetry has very little to say about the world we live in. The American poet is content to have a style that sets him apart, to produce a unique sound, to create unusual images. But in my poems I have been attempting to explore ordinary, everyday life with the aim of showing that it can be deep, that though the life itself may not be poetic and, in fact, can be banal and sordid, yet it is the stuff of poetry, and the kind of poetry I believe to be most important—that which shows our common humanity.

In order to show this I have had to tell stories, and this places me in the tradition of the Jewish people who have illustrated virtues and vices by referring to the behavior of the people down the street. My model for this kind of writing has been the stories I was told by my mother and by Jews sitting around a table.

> At this point, the person telling the story
> would say, "This shocket-sailor
> was one of our relatives, a distant cousin."

> It was always so, they knew they could depend on it.
> Even if the story made no sense,
> the one in the story would be a relative—
> a definite connection with the family.

Another model has been the writers who told stories about the Old Country that is so much a part of the history of my people. The Russia described by Gogol and by Dostoevski, with its forests and plains, its villages and cities, is part of my birthright. The model I have had constantly in mind is not Jewish—but I find it hard not to think of Anton Chekhov as a Jew. He has the pathos, the sense of dispersal, the desire to bring things back together, and the humor, that are found in the best Jewish writers.

Here is the difficulty one falls into when one speaks of Jewish writing or the characteristics of any race or nation—one finds that they are shared by other races and nations. Nevertheless, there are certain qualities that, if not uniquely

Jewish, have been cultivated by Jews—they have found it necessary to cultivate them. One of these qualities is humor, the kind that turns a sad situation around so that we can see the comical side. The Jews have often been strangers to the place where they lived, and have learned to see their wishes as absurd. Out of this they have developed the humor that seems characteristically Jewish. This humor can change an intolerable situation in the twinkling of an eye into a magical cave in which words flit about and the darkness gleams with hidden riches.

Again, in this respect my poems are an anomaly. American poets, especially the avant-garde, are not notable for their humor. Some of them are facetious, but facetiousness is the furthest thing from the humor I have in mind that rises out of our common humanity. My model for this kind of writing in verse would be Geoffrey Chaucer. But Chaucer was not a Jew, as Chekhov was not a Jew. As I have said, we run into difficulties if we try to ascribe certain characteristics to a race or nation. The difficulties vanish if we do not try to establish a claim, to stake out the ground in the name of this people or that. It is a matter of cultivation rather than of proprietorship. The humor I have named is not uniquely Jewish, but Jews have cultivated it.

Jews have no exclusive claim on writing with a sense of purpose, of design, a feeling for the hidden meaning of experience, and they have no monopoly on humor. But they have preserved these qualities, as they themselves have been preserved.

A Beach in Normandy,
a Bench at the Sorbonne

In Jamaica where I was born I had a very good teacher of French. His name was Wiehen, so I suppose he came from Alsace-Lorraine. He taught us Racine, Molière, Beaumarchais, and an unreadable book by Léon Blum of which I recollect only the phrase "minister without portfolio." We were schoolboys, we lived in the tropics, and we had never seen a portfolio. To this day I think of a minister looking for his portfolio which he has lost somewhere . . . on the Métro perhaps.

At the age of seventeen I left Jamaica and went to New York where I studied at Columbia University. I had a teacher of French there named Clamens. He was a small, serious man with a great admiration for Flaubert. He used to tell the story of the man who asked about a work of literature, "What purpose does it serve?" The answer, and the professor would deliver it with an air of triumph, was, "It serves to be beautiful." But the answer was not as final as he seemed to think; to this day I have been haunted by the question.

In 1943 I entered the U.S. Army, and after a period of training was assigned to the 101st Airborne Division. I was on the beach at Normandy on D Day, the sixth of June. My

This essay, translated into French by Serge Fauchereau, first appeared in *Paris-New York: Échanges littéraires au vingtième siècle,* edited by Serge Fauchereau (Paris: Bibliothèque Publique d'Information, Centre National d'Art et de Culture Georges Pompidou, 1977).

regiment was trained to use gliders, but on this occasion we came in by the sea and made our way inland among the hedgerows. Our first taste of actual combat was on the outskirts of Carentan. I can see every detail of the scene as clearly as if it were present: the lane with trees among which we were pinned down by German machine guns and mortars . . . the tree a few feet away being raked by bullets.

In the weeks that followed I came to know the soil of France intimately. Moreover, as I spoke the language I was frequently required to see what some Frenchman wanted, as he came toward us. Usually it was to tell us where the Germans were, and to ask us to spare his house. The military business would end with negotiations of a different kind . . . our cigarettes for their cognac. There was a great deal of friendship between the French and the Americans in those days.

Our division was used in the unsuccessful attempt to turn the German flank at Arnhem. After that we were sent to Rheims for rest and refitting. I remember one day going for a walk by myself in order to read a book and smoke my pipe. I found a shady hollow . . . when I looked along it, I realized that I was sitting in a trench of the First World War. When I was a boy in Jamaica I had read about that war—to be sitting in a trench of that war, thirty years later, filled me with strange thoughts. This is the kind of thing that is important to poets, and a few years later I wrote a poem titled "I Dreamed that in a City Dark as Paris," in which I imagined myself standing in the boots of a poilu.

> I dreamed that in a city dark as Paris
> I stood alone in a deserted square.
> The night was trembling with a violet
> Expectancy. At the far edge it moved
> And rumbled; on that flickering horizon
> The guns were pumping color in the sky.

The poem evokes the image of the poilu.

> The helmet with its vestige of a crest,
> The rifle in my hands, long out of date,
> The belt I wore, the trailing overcoat
> And hobnail boots . . .

The poem ends with the thought that his life had been interchanged with mine, and that these wars, in the effect they have had on the human imagination, have disrupted the old order of history and chronology. Life has become like a dream where anything is possible.

> The violence of waking life disrupts
> The order of our death. Strange dreams occur
> For dreams are licensed as they never were.

In December we went to Bastogne, and a few weeks later I found myself in a hospital in Paris. I had frozen feet and was supposed to stay in bed . . . but not likely! I wrote myself a pass and limped out to see Paris.

At the end of the war the regiment was stationed in Sens, and I was made the managing editor of the regimental newspaper published by a French press in Sens. I became a good friend of the publisher and his charming daughter. They were on short rations, but they invited me to their house and were most hospitable.

Every few days our newspaper staff would discover that we were running short of paper and that a trip to Paris was imperative. So we set off at dawn with a truck and returned to Sens at night with the big rolls of paper. In between we would have drunk our way from the bottom to the top of Montmartre.

I came back to France in 1948 and registered as a student at the University of Paris. This was disillusioning: the professors treated the Americans like children because we did not have a perfect grasp of French grammar and pronunciation. We wished to discuss literature, but we would be interrupted. . . . It was impossible to discuss anything intelligently.

In order to escape this atmosphere—courses intended for foreign students—I set out to register in a course in Baudelaire that was being offered in the university proper, that is, where the French students were. I imagined that I would be allowed to study as I liked and not be asked to contort my mouth in order to utter the vowels correctly. But when I arrived at the top of the stairs there was a man in a white coat holding a hypodermic needle. He informed me that this was an institution of the State and therefore I must be injected. He gave me an injection in the back, and I returned to my hotel and ran a fever. But thank God, it lasted only a few days. So I returned to the university to finish registering, only to be confronted once more by the doctor, who informed me that two more injections were required. Again I ran a fever. I did not return for the third injection, and to this day my knowledge of Baudelaire is imperfect. . . .

I had a friend named Allan Temko who was writing a book about the cathedral of Notre Dame. We both left the university and did our studies in the cafés around St.-Germain-des-Prés. At the end of my year in France I had a book of poems. It was privately printed by Union of Paris . . . unfortunately I cannot recollect the name of the printer. It cost only $500 in those days to print five hundred copies. Today a single copy of *The Arrivistes* is quoted by rare-book dealers at $350.

I have returned to France for short visits, and I am still interested in French literature. I have published translations of Apollinaire, and I frequently refer to French authors.

American poets have read French poetry—Eliot, Pound, William Carlos Williams, Hart Crane, Stevens, Cummings, and a number of poets writing at the present time, all have been strongly influenced by French poetry. It is time for French poets to know something about the United States.

The Poet and the Reader

words disappear *(handwritten margin note)*

Drury: In an essay you wrote for *The New Naked Poetry* you said that ideally the words of a poem should disappear from the page. How contradictory is that to Robert Graves's remark that poetry should "stand out in relief"?

Simpson: Absolute contradiction to what I'm talking about. As a matter of fact, I think in American poetry there is a big division now between the poets to whom language is a reality in itself—I would say that Ashbery is such a writer, and Wallace Stevens was such a writer—and the thing I'm talking about, which is a way of writing in which your attention is directed *through* the writing to the object you're talking about. You should be having the feeling, seeing the object, having the experience and not being immersed in the language itself. I'm not saying that's a bad way to write, the other way. I'm saying that I think a writer has to choose between these two extreme positions.

feeling over language *(handwritten margin note)*

Drury: Would it be fair to say that it's a difference between poems of surface and poems of content?

Simpson: Maybe so. I tend to think so. I think that Wallace Stevens is a poet of surface and that William Carlos Williams,

---

This interview first appeared in the *Iowa Journal of Literary Studies* 3, nos. 1 and 2 (University of Iowa, 1981). The interviewers were John Drury and Mark Irwin.

for example, is a poet of content. Of course, none of these things are absolutes. Obviously Williams paid attention to his language too, but the attention is not directed toward the style, it's being directed *through* style. The purpose of style is to make you experience the thing, not to experience the language itself.

Irwin: Would that also be like the narrative style of, say, a Russian novelist, someone like Gogol or Dostoevski, in which the reader becomes the narrator, becomes the persona? Do you want an invisible sort of surrender to the story?

Simpson: The object of any story is to get the person listening into it, into the experience. And you can use any technique that will make the person hearing forget that he's listening to a story, and actually feel that he's living the story. That's why Conrad and Ford were so involved in trying to find a plausible narrator, like Marlow. The object of that was to prevent the reader from being jarred all the time by the author telling him to look at this and look at that. The object of creating a narrator such as Marlow in *Lord Jim*, for example, is to give you the illusion that you're in a conversation where things are more acceptable. The problem of all storytelling is to set up a relationship between you and the reader, so that he believes the story. Now for my money, a very highly colored personal style tends to destroy that illusion, whereas in a style that is more—you may call it classical if you wish, or whatever, but I call it transparent—the words don't get in the way. There are levels, however, of possibility with language. I'm not arguing for simple, naive language. I'm arguing for language that is impersonal. *I*mpersonal. And therefore you don't feel that this is Louis Simpson telling you one of his stories, you feel, *gee, I can see the scene, I can get into it.* This is very opposed to the concept of the poet as a man who builds a peculiar style.

Irwin: So it's almost the same notion as when Proust talked about his writing as if watching from behind a glass door. I mean, that's the sort of impersonal tone you're talking about.

Simpson: Yes. I want detachment of the personal element from the work of art. You can't avoid the personal—I don't mean that—but you have to work your way through your own personality to get to a level that other people can share. It's that simple. For example, I read the poem "Typhus" last night, that poem about the young girl. Now if that appeared in a magazine without my name on it, I defy anybody to say that I wrote it. There are no mannerisms of style. Now some people may think, *well, but he's not much of a poet.* But that's a deliberate thing on my part. I want the story to be valid in terms of itself.

Drury: Except that other poets aren't working toward the same thing. In that sense it *is* individual, and it does stand out as an individual style.

Simpson: The only way they could say it might be Louis Simpson is because other people aren't writing that kind of subject. But there is a problem, because what I'm calling an impersonal style can sometimes sound close to prose. So the problem in writing these stories I've been writing is to maintain a very tight structure.

Irwin: It seems to me that in a pure notion of narrative poetry there is one inherent danger and that is if form begins to dictate the content then it could possibly rule out any sort of discovery or any lyricism that might happen in the poem itself. If one sets out to write a narrative poem and thinks always that this is a narrative poem, isn't that placing form before content?

Simpson: No, I don't think so. When you write a song you don't stop halfway through and start a meditative poem. Any poem you write has a kind of form that you accept and work within. Everything that you undertake to do has its own general outlines and you work within those outlines. Sometimes you can break the form quite plausibly in the middle of a poem. There's nothing to prevent you in the middle of a narrative poem from having a kind of chorus or some other sort of element come into the poem if you can manage it. No, there's great freedom of movement. Again, the point is what kind of effect you are trying to make, and every artist is conscious generally of the kind of effect he's trying to make. I'm arguing against subjective poetry that does not relate to the outer world and outer actions. I'm arguing against poetry which is—

Drury: Self indulgent?

Simpson: Well, you can give it all sorts of names, but the kind of poem that Anne Sexton wrote is the kind of thing that I think is a dead end.

Drury: That would be a particular danger in using the materials of autobiography.

Simpson: Yes, it is very dangerous.

Drury: Maybe that's the strongest reason to move toward the impersonal you're talking about.

Simpson: That's why I mentioned two of those people yesterday—Plath and Lowell—but you see I think that in their cases, as I said, the character in the poem is being used dramatically and being moved around. It's not a naked self-revelation.

Drury: Of course, if one isn't writing narrative poetry there would be the danger of going back to writing impersonal poems about impersonal subjects, like a lot of the poetry that came out of the New Criticism.

Simpson: Oh yes, there is the danger of writing a poem which is just a construction, but I always put the emphasis on the fact that the poem must convey some feeling and contact which they did not put an emphasis on. I don't by any means think that form alone can produce a poem.

Irwin: It seems that today there is a kind of poetry which wants to start not with anything concrete but with what might be notes toward a poem or something elliptical. How much do you think a poem can start to find its subject matter as it goes? Stevens does that to a certain extent in some of his poems: he'll start with an elliptical point and then move toward its center.

Simpson: You see, the main problem for writers of poetry is that there is no longer a common language of feeling. So the writers have become terribly self-conscious about speaking out on any subject and also about buttonholing the reader and saying, *I'm going to tell you a story, I'm going to give you this kind of poem.* So what writers try to do is slide into the subject in an informal, casual manner, or a manner that will be acceptable to the listener, who would not accept a story told straight out, and involve the reader in the difficulty of writing—that's what you're talking about. They involve the reader in the difficulty of having a voice, of beginning at any point in time, of making a plausible statement. They involve the reader in the actual writing of the story, so that at a certain point they can sort of cooperate with the reader, the reader cooperates with them, saying, *I understand that it's only a story, it's only fiction, but let's see what kind of a game this is and how we work it out.* Donald Barthelme carries that to an extreme. It's a sign of the lack of a language of feeling. We don't trust the reader, we don't know what he feels and what he cannot feel. So we try to say we're all writing this together, beginning with notes, beginning with random observations. Kind of a cooperative effort. And the excuse for it is that this is the way the world is, therefore the writer must do likewise. A question was raised to me the other day: a man said there were so many voices, how can you possibly choose one? There may be any number of voices but you as a writer can do anything you like—you can choose one. I'm a little turned off by the fragmentation and the note beginnings and the elliptical thing you're talking about—because I want to get a charge of feeling or scene going in a story and I don't want to waste my time with that. At the same time I do want the reader to accept what I'm saying, so the main problem for me has been to develop a writing voice that I can apply, a plausible style in which I can tell a story, a style that moves straight forward but still sounds like the way people might think. It's very difficult because the tendency is to fall into prose. So again I come back to the happening, the actual structure of the story itself, because that prevents its being prose. As long as people are listening intently it's a poem, I think.

Drury: How conscious are you of where a poem is going and where it will end? Is there still a lot of the process of discovery involved in it?

Simpson: Oh, yes. I have a lot of trouble with poems. I don't usually have trouble starting them, or even working through the middle parts, but the endings are always the devil. Because I know there is something important happening, but exactly what direction to go in is the problem. I spend a lot of time rewriting and leaving things to sit and gel and come back and ask myself over and over again what direction. I've often changed a story. I thought it was going to go one way and then had it move in another direction, and often as a result of reading it to someone or having them read it. An acute reader is the best friend a narrative poet can have. In fact, a narrative poet *needs* a couple of people that he can trust who will say, *well, that just doesn't work.*

Drury: I would imagine it would be much easier in a discursive, associative poem to get away with all sorts of things.

Simpson: Well yeah, that's the point. There's a kind of poem that is written all the time: descriptive poetry or poetry that is discursive and just doesn't go anywhere. It doesn't make anything happen. A lot of ideas we have can be written out as verse, but that doesn't make something real happen, and a lot of poetry is just a man's thoughts, or a woman's thinking. And for me that's not even the beginning of art. We're walking around all day long with a lot of thoughts. Until a man starts to make something happen in a kind of structure that is a poem, for me he hasn't begun to be a poet. I see long poems, descriptions of—I don't know—one thing or another. They aren't even the beginning of a poem. They're lifeless, they have no movement, they have no action, they have no vitality of themselves. In a funny sense what I'm looking for is a kind of folk art for American intellectuals. Really. I want a folk art. People who go to universities do have a background which is a kind of common, shared, "folk" background—we've all read the same books, and so on. And I'm asking for a kind of poem that is a happening, not a poem which is just a discussion.

Drury: So it wouldn't be enough for a poem to be simply a "graph of the mind."

Simpson: It has to be a drama of some kind.

Irwin: You have a way of making what is antitragic sort of tragic. I think of your poem "The True Weather for Women." What I want to ask is how impersonal you think the voice becomes. If I were to compare some of your endings, they all seem strong, but they're flat, in the way a Rousseau painting is flat. If there were a great folk voice it could never impede itself, it would always be an open voice, or maybe a loud echo.

Simpson: I try to leave my poems at the end with a kind of openness about them. I never try to finish them.

Drury: They do seem to dissolve into a kind of resonance.

Simpson: Yes. That's what I want.

Drury: I was wondering if the use of meditation in reconstructing scenes would have something to do with that, if the act of meditating doesn't inhabit the poem when it's written, too, and give it that resonance.

Simpson: I think so. I think that such meditation as I have done has made me think about a thing more and more deeply. But it's a *real* thing, it's a situation, and you can imagine it and meditate upon it until something moves, and you write your action. You can make up things, but they have to become realities, psychological realities, for you, and then you can work with them. An imaginary scene can be just as real as a scene in your own life, because it involves your own feelings and ideas.

Irwin: Would you agree that if true narrative poetry could be viewed as a horizontal movement—in other words, a movement from A to B—that lyrical poetry, on the other hand, would be a constant vertical movement, as in a poem by Dylan Thomas where the first line is heavy with both the overture and the sequel?

Simpson: Well, it may be true of Dylan Thomas.

Irwin: If the poem ever falls anyplace in the movement, it seems as though it could not be written.

Simpson: Well no, it couldn't afford to fall. A lyrical movement can't falter. But lyrical movements can be just sheer repetition, they can be waves of the same thing over and over again, like a Burns lyric, a restatement of the same thing. And some of Thomas: "The Force That Through the Green Fuse Drives the Flower" is a poem which simply repeats the same idea four or five times. The difference between a lyrical poem and a narrative poem would simply be that the narrative poem is telling you a story and that the prime object of a lyrical poem is to release a kind of feeling. The narrative poem is trying to tell you something about the experience, the way people live or think. It can be very subtle. I don't want it to sound as though I'm now arguing for simple stories. They can be very subtle indeed.

Irwin: How about someone like Seamus Heaney? Does he seem like a good example of lyric and narrative, equally balanced?

Simpson: Yes, he does. Some of his narratives become meditations. That seems to be one of the hardest—to join the two, to get an equal balance between the two. There just aren't many poets that fall into that. What bothers me is a few kinds of American poetry being written. One is a little teeny bitty anecdote that doesn't matter much. That's not really what I call a narrative poem. And another is a kind of travelogue. Actually, last night while I was reading to the audience, I was thinking, *well now, here is a group of poems about Australia, here I've read them a couple of poems about this imaginary Russia.* Am I just a dilettante in travel? No, there has to be behind all those poems a cohesive voice, a cohesive point of view which would make a book. The new book I've made is held together by a point of view that's behind all those poems. Every one of the poems is looking for an emotional effect; there must be a resemblance between those emotional effects, and that's what's really holding the book together, what I'm calling the voice.

Drury: Do you see the new book as a kind of companion piece to *Searching for the Ox,* or as very different?

Simpson: Not very different, but it's not a companion piece—it moves on from that. All books are transitional, I suppose, but there was a weakness in the *Searching for the Ox* book. Not the title poem, I'm very pleased with the title poem. But with quite a few of the other poems, I feel in looking back on it, while I had a story and I was trying to tell it, the structure was not quite charged enough at all points, or came too close to prose. Which was not true of the book before, *Adventures of the Letter I,* which was more highly colored and more poetic in the traditional sense. Some of the flatnesses of the book *Searching for the Ox* have been worked out by me in this present book. I think the poems in this book are not poetic in language the way that some of the poems in *Adventures of the Letter I* were, but in this book the structure of the poems is more sure, and the tension is maintained more strongly. And also I've done more daring things in the narratives in this book, in terms of conversations and simply taking a room with people in it and seeing if you can make a poem out of people in a room. A very hard thing to do. Just a domestic scene, and so on. I think it works in this book better. I think maybe the voice is surer than it was. I think the last poem in the book, the most recent poem I've written, is really very successful in terms of making a bunch of people sit around and talk, and then, from that, moving out through the mind of one of the characters into a jungle scene, and then back into the room. That kind of risk I did not take in the *Searching for the Ox* book. And I think it works wonderfully, and within my definition of realism it's perfectly legitimate because I'm moving through the mind of one of the characters.

Irwin: You have a wonderful talent for a tragic-comic vision— in the way you've taken the line from the Chekhov story for the new title . . .

Simpson: Caviare at the Funeral.

Irwin: Would it be true that you share a tragic-comic vision in the way that Joyce would see that in anything tragic there's really a comic notion in it?

Simpson: I think so. The kind of writing I like most is that kind of mixture. I think that some of the greatest humorous writing is like that. Chaucer is like that, Shakespeare is like that. I think the Henry IV plays are terribly tragic if you think about them, really, from one point of view, but they *are* funny as hell too. Falstaff *is* the great comic character, right? I think he's a tragic character too. After all, this is very deeply embedded in literature, this tradition of the mixture. In Greek literature, in Hebrew literature, surely, you find this mixture. I don't think it's true, however, of Dante. Except in maybe a couple of spots where he *looks* at it—like the Paolo and Francesca episode. But in general his view of life is that it is divine *comedy*, in the sense that you're supposed to go out laughing. You're supposed to go laughing through hell, really, because this is an example of God's beautiful justice. But I want a mixture of pathos—real pathos, not the violin strings trembling—but I love the sense of something being very enjoyable and yet rather sad too. Of course, there are certain things that cannot be treated this way, certain episodes that are just too ghastly for words. You see that little poem I read about the man who came back from prison? The first version was two pages long, and I had it in a cell in prison, and I had a description in the poem of a man who had been beaten to death, coming back into the cell and dying in front of him—which had actually happened. But the poem couldn't sustain it. It would either have had to be a hell of a lot longer, and circumstantial, and much more detailed, or else you had to leave that out. So my main point in the poem—and after all I had to decide what *was* my main point—was that he had been in prison, he was back in ordinary life, and we're all like that, we're all very ordinary, even the people who've been to prison and been through terrible experiences. "He glances at the magazine, / looking through the table of contents." And that was the real, subtle point of the original poem. And the other stuff about the man being beaten to death in the cell and so on was something that other people had written, or could write better. It could be imagined; we don't have to go through all that. These are points that you come to by your own meditation, and by thinking—about art, you know. While you're working, you're really going through a very intense intellectual discipline, when you write a poem. I don't know of any discipline so exhausting, really, as that kind of questioning of yourself:

What do I want to do? Why am I doing this? Why is this dead? What is missing? Is there another way entirely of approaching this? A poet is involved in this thought all the time—that is, if he's a working poet. A lot of poets stop working. What is tragic about American poets, one after another, is that they learn how to write a certain level style. And it's like a man who learns to skate: they simply glide on that level forever and ever. What was good about the work was the *sense* of struggle and creation when they were younger, and then it stops, and you get a kind of performance that doesn't matter very much. I've always changed, and it's been a problem for me in terms of reputation. But it doesn't matter to me about that. The fact is that people don't know where to have me, they don't know what to do with me. What am I up to, or don't I know? What I'm up to is actual involvement with the process itself all the time. Which makes for some failures, real failures. There are always a handful of poems I've published in my books that are just failures: four or five or six. But I think the kind of narrative I'm learning to write comes out of taking a lot of real risks. I've been trying to render experience directly . . . unadorned. There's a way of saying things directly, you know. There is a way of saying the right thing. And also being poetic about it.

Irwin: Truthful.

Simpson: Yeah. The poetry resides, as Wilfred Owen said, in the truth. The poetry's in the pity, he said. That's a great statement. It doesn't mean that you're not going to have problems with language or structure. God knows, from what I've said you must understand how hard I think about this whole thing. But it does mean that you can't bamboozle the reader with just sheer erudition.

Irwin: It seems that this truth you're talking about, this simple and candid truth—there's a poem by Donald Hall called "The Ox-Cart Man."

Simpson: I think that's a remarkable poem.

Irwin: How he builds the cart, takes his produce, sells the thing, and starts over.

Simpson: You know something? It's a very interesting idea, but he *did* it very well, he carried it off very well.

Irwin: It's a very ambitious poem, but he makes the occasion seem small, which almost doubles its reach.

Simpson: I think it's the best thing he's ever written. If I were doing an anthology of contemporary poetry I would put that in without question. You know, Williams's remark was that as long as you're involved with the technique of writing you're OK. And I believe that more and more as I get older. I said that to someone and they thought I meant something very trivial. Technique for me involves feeling, it involves everything.

Drury: How do you feel about your early poems, when you were writing in traditional forms?

Simpson: I don't read them any more. I don't deny them. There are one or two I still read. The poem "Carentan O Carentan"—the war poems I still read. For one reason, I think that the traditional form was very well suited to some of that material.

Drury: What about "The Runner?"

Simpson: No, I don't read that.

Drury: Well, it's much longer.

Simpson: And it's blank verse. I think that it was the wrong form.

Drury: Would it work outside of its blank verse?

Simpson: Yes. I think if I were writing that story now I could write it in free verse very well. The kind of stuff that I was reading by Patrick Kavanagh, that kind of moving, free line. There's nothing to prevent you writing in free verse and then going into rhyme at certain points if you feel like clinching something. Lowell does it in *Life Studies* very well—he uses rhyme now and then in a kind of playful manner and a kind of echo.

Drury: Well, Kavanagh was rhymed, the part you were reading.

Simpson: Parts of it. There's nothing to prevent you doing anything you like. No, the early poems I don't deal with now because I am not interested in the kind of thing I was trying to say—or mainly the kind of mood I was trying to create, a kind of dancing meter in many places—whereas now I'm much closer to my own voice when I write. I'm listening to my own voice speaking, really. But much more concentrated. I love it when I can get out of my own voice into the voices of other people. I know this is not a poetry reading, but can I read you part of that poem I was talking about? It's called "The Man She Loved" and it begins, you see, in an impersonal narrative:

> In the dusk
> men with sidelocks, wearing hats
> and long black coats walked side by side,
> hands clasped behind their backs,
> talking Yiddish. It was like being in a foreign country.
>
> The members of the family
> arrived one by one . . .
> his aunts, his uncle, and his mother
> talking about her business
> in Venezuela. She had moved to a new building
> with enough space and an excellent location.

Now here you're running very close to prose. You have to be very careful. But if it's tight enough, and the language has a certain . . . The words "She had moved to a new building / with enough space and an excellent location"—the "l" sounds are working here, you know.

Irwin: Right. But it seems also that the reason you couldn't be reading fiction is that there's always a subtle rhetorical tone. Would you say that's part of it?

Simpson: Yes. Let me go on:

> To their simple, affectionate questions
> he returned simple answers.
> For how could he explain what it meant to be a writer . . .
> a world that was entirely different,
> and yet it would include the sofa
> and the smell of chicken cooking.

I'm having *fun* with these poems! And it's myself in the poem, but I've got a distance between me and that guy, which is quite large. And then—

> Little did they know as they spoke
> that one day they would be immortal
> in a novel that commanded the sweep
> of Tolstoy. . .

I don't know if you remember in a poem called "Sway"—at the end of the poem when he says he's going to be a novelist. And this guy is *me*, but he's a failed novelist, you see. The guy writing these narrative poems is a failed novelist. It's kind of a joke in the book:

> in a novel that commanded the sweep
> of Tolstoy, a magnificent creation
> that would bring within its compass
> offices in Manhattan and jungles
> of the Amazon. A grasp of . . .

He's reviewing his own novel!

> A grasp of psychology
> and sense of the passing of time
> that one can only compare to,
> without exaggerating, Proust.

I had a *lovely* time writing that sentence. You see? I'm not sure that people will get it. And then he goes right into this daydream—and he's sitting in the room with these other people, right?

> The path wound through undergrowth.
> Palms rose at an angle from the humid plain.
> He passed a hut with chickens and goats . . .
> an old man who sat with his back to a wall,
> not seeing. A woman came out of a door
> and stared after him.
> In the distance
> the purple mountains shone, fading
> as the heat increased.

Clear out of that room—into a Conradian *Nostromo*. It's triggered, however, by the Venezuelan reference that came eighteen lines before. I think you can play, you can have a lot of fun with it. Then suddenly:

> "Let me take a look at it,"
> said Joey. He took the watch
> from Beth, pried open the back,
> and laid it on the table before him.
> Then from the pocket of his vest
> he produced a jeweler's loupe.
> He screwed this into his eye
> and examined the works.
> "I can fix it. It only needs an adjustment."

You see the shift in the poem, from that dream world back. . . . Now, that's what I mean by the kind of problems and the kind of stuff you can do. And I'm enjoying it.

Irwin: Maybe some of the public's difficulty with reading poetry like this would be the subtlety and the shift of tonalities. It seems that the contemporary notion is to shock the reader with the unexpected and get all the orgiastic things out of the way.

Simpson: As a writer you must assume one thing which is very hard to assume: that people are listening . . . with great attention. Now today this is almost a madman's idea—I mean, to think that people are listening to poetry with *real* attention, and hearing that kind of shift, is almost—you have to be crazy to believe it. Because they can't even hear—I mean my students (I'm sure that's true here too), a lot of them can't hear the most *blunt* voices, much less these shifts. However, whenever you start to feel a little desperate about that, imagine when Conrad was writing: who was hearing the shifts in *his* narratives, or who was discovering the things that graduate students now are studying and discovering? Who was *aware* of that in his own time? When he was publishing serial stories in *Blackwood's,* how many of those readers were aware of the subtlety . . .

Irwin: Or Proust, who was taking twice the distance . . .

Simpson: Yes. But every artist—this is the secret of a real artist—assumes that absolute attention is out there somewhere. Now this is what makes you work. It's out there somewhere. Someday, someone will read this poem and really get it. That's what your audience is, that belief. Somewhere out there is an audience. Listening. And will pay attention to *why* you didn't use this word or chose that word instead. And the curious thing is that the people that have that belief, that faith, find the audience. Proust said they create it. And you do, in a way. You create the audience that can read you.

Beauty—A Footnote to Plato

Ortega y Gasset observed that "No one can estimate the penetration of concepts of ancient philosophy into the ranks of western civilization. The most uneducated man uses words and concepts from Plato, Aristotle, and the Stoics."

The influence Ortega had in mind derives from passages such as the following, in Plato's "Symposium," where Diotima speaks of love and beauty.

> the true order of going, or being led by another, to the things of love, is to begin from the beauties of earth and mount upwards for the sake of that other beauty, using these steps only, and from one going on to two, and from two to all fair forms, and from fair forms to fair practices, and from fair practices to fair notions, until from fair notions he arrives at the notion of absolute beauty, and at last knows what the essence of beauty is. This, my dear Socrates, . . . is that life above all others which man should live, in the contemplation of beauty absolute.

When paganism made way for Christianity the concept of an absolute beauty was retained, the Madonna replacing the Venus of Milo. Then a new faith appeared on the scene—by the end of the eighteenth century philosophy was claiming to have overthrown Christianity and established the age of Reason. But the arguments of Reason could not control the will-to-power of a Robespierre or Napoleon; after Waterloo a gen-

This essay first appeared in *Soundings* 20 (Stony Brook, New York, Spring 1983).

eration disillusioned with philosophy turned to making money.

There was an alternative, however: you could believe in Art, the creation of beauty. To Baudelaire, beauty was "a dream in stone." Beauty was calm. Beauty was style—the expression of a personality that made everything serve its vision. The novelist Huysmans says of his hero, "The only thing that mattered to him was the writer's personality, and the only thing that interested him was the working of the writer's brain."

In the nineteenth century there was an apotheosis of the artist in literature, music, and painting. A Flaubert, a Wagner, a Van Gogh—each seemed to be striving to recreate the universe in his own style.

This was different from the beauty envisioned by Diotima. There the neophyte climbed a ladder, proceeding from the love of fair forms to fair practices, and from fair practices to fair notions, et cetera—a movement outward from the self to the universe, reaching after the Good. But the nineteenth-century religion of Art placed the source of beauty in the artist himself, his "genius." At the end of the century science reinforced this point of view: to the psychologist there were no truths external to the mind. There were no visions—only thoughts and dreams, which could be accounted for by examining the mind of the dreamer.

The word *beauty* has been in disrepute with intellectuals because it is vague or because it rubs their Puritanism the wrong way. (Once, in conversation with an American poet I used the word. His face altered like a Victorian parson's on hearing a four-letter word, and he said snappishly, "I want to write some decent stuff, that's all." But an Italian peasant has no compunction in saying that a scene or song is beautiful. In Ezra Pound's poem the children say of a woman or a fish, "*Ch' e be'a.*")

But things are changing. Physicists speak of a "big bang" that converted energy into matter and distributed it through the universe, every particle bearing a history of the whole, so that the universe, like Wordsworth's view of Alpine scenery, exhibits

> workings of one mind, the features
> Of the same face, blossoms upon one tree.

The universe may prove, after all, to have a design like a painting, symphony, or poem, of which our paintings, symphonies, and poems are reflections.

If science is giving us new visions we shall need a word to describe them. The technical jargon that passes for literary and aesthetic criticism—having no word to express our feelings we need a thousand words—cannot convey the excitement we feel when we perceive a thing that strikes us instantly as being true and, there is no other word, beautiful.

But our beauty will be different from Plato's—science has taught us that. Our own thought-processes are part of it. "We can no longer speak of the behavior of the particle independently of the process of observation."

The beauty Diotima glimpsed was changeless. Ours is changing, like the images in Yeats's "Byzantium":

> Those images that yet
> Fresh images beget,
> That dolphin-torn, that gong-tormented sea.

II

Poets and Writers

Honoring Whitman

He most honors my style who learns under it how to destroy the teacher.
"Song of Myself"

I began reading Whitman seriously around 1959. I had read him before that out of curiosity, but in 1959 I was changing from writing in regular meters and forms to writing in irregular meters and forms, and Whitman was one of the poets I read to see how they did it.

I liked the pictures in Whitman's poems: cavalry crossing a ford, a tree standing by itself. I liked his idea of a "Muse install'd amid the kitchenware," i.e., making poetry out of common things. This seemed useful in view of the part played by machinery in our lives a hundred years later.

On the other hand, his whooping it up over the chest-expansion of the United States didn't do a thing for me. His wish for young men to throw their arms about his neck struck me as incomprehensible. I was put off by his use of big-sounding words or French words. He was capable of writing long passages naming countries he'd read about or heard about, the names of mountains and rivers, the races of men, et cetera.

> I see the Brazilian vaquero,
> I see the Bolivian ascending mount Sorata. . . .

This essay first appeared in *Walt Whitman: The Measure of His Song,* edited by Jim Perlman, Ed Folsom, and Dan Campion (Minneapolis: Holy Cow! Press, 1981).

I don't see how anyone could ever have read these passages in Whitman with pleasure.

At times, however, he was capable of a surprising compression of thought and style—he was almost epigrammatic: "The nearest gnat is an explanation," "Trippers and askers surround me."

On the whole I found Whitman exhilarating. His freedom of line and style, and his interest in pots and pans, bringing them over into poetry, were what I needed at the time.

So far I haven't mentioned Whitman's "philosophy." It consists of two or three ideas. One, it is possible to merge in your feelings with others, and it is possible for others to merge in their feelings with you. Two, if this occurs over a distance, or over a span of time, it seems to annihilate space and time. This is a kind of immortality. Three, in order to convey your feelings to others you must, by a process of empathic observation, using all your senses, take things into yourself and express them again. The senses are "dumb ministers" of feeling . . . through them we know one another. The poet is the manager of this process—he puts what we feel and see into words.

These ideas, which can be found in "There Was a Child Went Forth" and "Crossing Brooklyn Ferry," are the substratum of Whitman's thinking. This is quite enough for a poet to go on. Poets don't have to be philosophers on the scale of Kant—they need only have ideas that enable them to make sense out of their experience and make it seem worthwhile to go on writing. They don't need to be original—the first ambition of those who are profoundly unoriginal. It isn't so hard to be original—it's a sight harder to say something true and useful.

It may appear that I've overlooked Whitman's mystical, visionary side. I haven't overlooked it, but Whitman doesn't strike me as mystical or visionary—he is a naturalist first and last. He wills to see things—even "The Sleeper" is laid out and proceeds according to plan. His most ecstatic passages are descriptions of sexual intercourse or frottation.

> I mind how once we lay such a transparent summer
>   morning,
> How you settled your head athwart my hips and gently
>   turn'd over upon me . . . .

These lines are addressed to his soul, but can there be any doubt as to what is actually happening? Sex may be the link with a mystery, but at least let us see that it is sex and not rush to find an alternative explanation. There is the kind of reader who, having no knowledge of religion, is always looking in books for the secret of the universe. For such a one, Whitman will be mystic, together with Kahlil Gibran and the authors of pamphlets on astrology.

Insofar as Whitman enthuses over "a great round wonder rolling in space" he is a rudimentary poet, the eternal sophomore enthusing over "the great ideas" and neglecting his physics lesson and his French. Insofar as Whitman talks about the universe he is not worth the attention of a grown person.

On the other hand, when he looks at what he sees, he is certainly a great American poet (though he cannot stand comparison with Dante, Chaucer, or a dozen others). These are the passages to look for:

> The little one sleeps in its cradle,
> I lift the gauze and look a long time, and silently brush away
>   flies with my hand.
>
> The youngster and the red-faced girl turn aside up the
>   bushy hill,
> I peeringly view them from the top . . . .
>
>   ("Song of Myself")

> Through the ample open door of the peaceful country barn,
> A sunlit pasture field with cattle and horses feeding,
> And haze and vista, and the far horizon fading away.
>   ("A Farm Picture")

I don't want to suggest that Whitman is only a picture-artist. "When Lilacs Last in the Dooryard Bloom'd" and "Out of the

Cradle Endlessly Rocking" hold our attention through rhythm and sound as well as imagery. But as rhythm and sound are operating just as audibly in his empty, monotonous, forgettable poems, I do not think that Whitman's impressiveness depends on rhythm and sound. It is what he describes that makes him a poet. Rhythm and sound are only an aid to this.

Critics who wish to pore over a phrase in Whitman, or the structure of a line, and show how perfectly suited it is to his purpose, should choose a banality and show why the meter and phrasing are perfect. This is the trouble with criticism that concentrates on technique—it is an *arrière-pensée*. We know that the poetry is fine, and set about finding reasons why the meter and the syntax had to be just so. But these things in themselves do not make fine poetry. If nothing worthwhile is being said, meter, syntax, and the rest of the prosodist's and the grammarian's bag of tricks are so much useless baggage.

There are ranges of poetry that lie beyond Whitman. Of situations such as occur in people's lives he appears to have known very little, and these are our main concern. He is good at describing shipwrecks, which are infrequent, but does not show affections, attachments, anxieties, shades of feeling, passions . . . the life we actually have. The human appears in his poems as a crowd or as a solitary figure . . . himself, looking at others.

In recent years there has been talk by American poets of developing new kinds of consciousness which would, presumably, enable us to advance beyond the merely human. But it is self-evident that if we are to continue to exist it will be as human beings, not some other species. Our poets are trying to be like stones . . . another way of saying that they would rather be dead. Paul Breslin made the point clearly in an article ("How to Read the New Contemporary Poem," *American Scholar*, Summer 1978) but the thought had occurred to me independently. According to Breslin, our poets of darkness and stones are trying to escape the consequences of being human. They are trying to cast out the ego and live in a Jungian universe of archetypes.

Readers of this kind will find Whitman reassuring—he never becomes involved. "I am the man," he states, "I suffer'd, I was there." The passage may be so well known because it is so refreshing, in the wasteland of his usual detachment. He is a stroller, an onlooker, a gazer, and has nothing to say about what goes on in the houses he is passing, or behind office or factory windows, or in the life of the man turning a plough. He does not seem to know what people say to each other— especially what men say to women, or women to men. Reading Whitman's poetry one would think that the human race is dumb—and indeed, as he tells us, he would rather turn and live with animals.

His poetry is about a spectacle . . . a crowd on the ferry, "the fine centrifugal spokes of light round the shape of my head in the sunlit water." But the actualities of human society are a closed book to him. It isn't the "proud libraries" that are closed to him—indeed, at times we could wish they were. What is closed is the life of the individual, and the lives of two, and three.

Whitman has plenty to say about man "*En-Masse*." His optimism about the common man reflects the optimism of the bankers and railroad-builders in the Gilded Age. Man "*En-Masse*" provided them with labor and then with a mass-market. But optimism about the masses seems out of place in our century. The masses elect mass-murderers—if we survive it will not be due to the good nature of the common man. Whitman's view of mankind is of no use at all—it doesn't help when it comes to understanding one another and building a community.

As he has so little to say about actual circumstances, Whitman is not among the very great, realized poets. There is hardly any drama or narration in his poetry—ideas aren't realized in action. We rise from reading Whitman with the feeling that he has talked about life rather than created it.

Building on his achievement we may hope to do much better, as he himself, in one of his generous moods, said that we would.

The Poet-Maker

The effect Whitman has upon his readers is described in his poem "Song of the Answerer":

> The words of the true poems give you more than poems,
> They give you to form for yourself poems . . .

It is like the saying that has been going around recently: if you give a man a fish you only feed him for a day—if you teach him to fish you feed him for a lifetime. Whitman intends to make poets of his readers rather than give them perfectly realized poems. He doesn't satisfy our appetite for story and drama—instead, he encourages us to make our own.

This first appeared in *West Hills Review* 3 (Huntington Station, New York, 1981–82).

The Originality of Wordsworth

Much of your narrative poetry of the last twenty years is based on the rhythms of speech. Was this influenced by Wordsworth, who comments in his Preface to Lyrical Ballads *that he wants to describe situations from common life in a selection of language really used by men?*

Yes. Wordsworth is very much on my mind. Every time I've made a statement to the effect that I write with the sound of speech in my ear, I always think of that Preface by Wordsworth. It is the touchstone of that way of writing poetry.

Do you mean a narrative poetry about characters other than yourself?

No. I'm speaking about the language of poetry now, which could apply in a lyric, or in narrative, or meditative verse.

The Preface is misleading if you take it as a prescription for Wordsworth's practice all the time. There are some passages of the *The Prelude* which are by no means simple speech. Of course, the whole question that Coleridge raises is a very

---

This interview first appeared in the *Wordsworth Circle* 13, no. 2 (Spring 1982). The interviewer was Steven Schneider, Temple University. My editor says that the writing is loose and urges me to tighten up the piece. But this was a conversation and the value of such things is in their spontaneity. Some writers revise their "interviews" so that they read like essays. I don't hold with this, and have allowed the interview to stand as it occurred.

important one. He really got Wordsworth philosophically on that. When Coleridge says that in order to select the language of poetry from the language used by men, you must already have what you think is the language of poetry in your head before you make the selection.

However, to get back to your point, I do think of that passage by Wordsworth, and I use that kind of language in lyrical writing or in narrative. I think one has to stay in touch with the dramatic quality of language.

The issue of using the rhythms of common speech has come up before in American poetry. Williams has remarked similarly, and even before Williams, Whitman tried to speak in what he thought was the common language of the time. Can we say that Wordsworth's choosing the rhythms of common speech has been assimilated by these other poets as well?

Not consciously. In the two cases you mention, Whitman and Williams, there is no evidence, that I can see, that either of them had read Wordsworth carefully. I would be quite sure they had not. Williams doesn't mention Wordsworth in his writing or letters that I can remember. He mentions Keats, but not Wordsworth. Of course, Whitman would have got Wordsworth by way of American poets writing in the nineteenth century, men like Bryant, who were heavily influenced by Wordsworth.

A section of your book, Searching for the Ox, *is entitled "The Company of Flesh and Blood." Is that whole section inspired by Wordsworth's line from the 1802 Preface, "I have wished to keep the reader in the company of flesh and blood"?*

No. It's not inspired by Wordsworth's line. I was working in a direction which I saw was similar to Wordsworth's. I found the quotation in Wordsworth and applied it to my own work.

In other words, you were already working in that direction when you came across the quotation.

Oh, yes. I think that's how it works for most people. They're working in a certain direction. Then they find an author who is sympathetic, an established author, and they can take something from him.

If we can go one step further, what is in sympathy in that section of poems between yours and Wordsworth's work?

It's very much the question of basing poetry in experience and in common life. It's that simple. Many poets, you know, especially in contemporary American poetry, search for the most farfetched images, the most farfetched situations, or they don't even have situations in their poetry. They really philosophize a great deal or produce images not rooted in any human situation. They may have a style which is striking, or like a kind of music of their own, but it does not evoke human life. I have been putting a lot of people into my poems and a lot of human situations. They're very dramatic.

In American Poets *(1976), edited by William Heyen, your essay "Rolling Up" praises Wordsworth for moving to the lakes and mountains to create imaginary men. What exactly did you mean by that, and do you think poets ought to do that?*

Wordsworth's case was political. He was, as everyone knows, very disillusioned by the French Revolution as it turned toward Robespierre. Then he was appalled by the British declaration of war on France and the consequences of that. He felt, as he says in *The Prelude,* as though he were a traitor among his own people. Right? So he withdrew from politics really. Up to that point, as he says in *The Prelude,* he had hailed the Revolution. In a sense, I suppose he felt he had made a terrible mistake, and he says so.

In getting involved with politics in the first place?

Yes. He had made a terrible mistake in buying the ideas of the Philosophes, the French materialist philosophers of the Enlightenment, men like Diderot who really did believe that the world was going to be perfected through a combination of political enlightenment and science. And of course in reading Godwin, even more so. Wordsworth read Godwin, and Godwin had a systematized view of life and society. Now, as Wordsworth says in *The Prelude*, he became disillusioned with all this, so he withdrew physically from the center of fashionable, intellectual life, the intellectual life of the avant-garde of his time, which would have been Godwin and later on Shelley. Wordsworth withdrew physically and mentally from London and went to live in this place which was isolated.

Now, when I say he made up a race of people, this is true. He did not find those characters around him. After all, peasant life is not as noble as he presents it as being.

I'm not saying that Wordsworth misrepresented that life, but he certainly gave it more dignity and philosophic weight than it has to the everyday eye. He created a fictional race. He created the Cumberland beggar. He did see an old beggar. He did see an old man gathering leeches, but by the time Wordsworth was through with the old man gathering leeches, he was a lot more than any old man gathering leeches. He becomes a waterfall, a torrent, a rock, whatever. So, it is a fictional race.

Picking up on Wordsworth's disillusionment with politics, would you say he shifted his attention from the outward sphere, toward the imagination, hoping he could change the lives of his readers through poetry?

Yes. I think that's very true. I think that from being a believer in the possibility of social revolution, as so many young men and women are, he moved simply to the idea that the revolution had to occur from within.

In that same essay you wrote that Blake was a poet for the sixties in America, whereas Wordsworth shows the way to the future. Can you elaborate more on this distinction?

Yes. In the 1960s there was a great deal of talk among young people of expanding one's consciousness, and Blake for many of them was taken to do just that. Blake turns his back very firmly upon the material world you see with the eye, and claims that you make up reality yourself. That's how I read Blake, and I think it's a right reading.

Knowledge is structured in consciousness?

That's right. We really do create the universe in our heads, and Blake's not joking. Now Wordsworth is quite unlike that. And you know that Blake condemned Wordsworth, or criticized him very severely, for insisting on nature, for Wordsworth's unremitting attention to what he actually saw and felt. Now the 1960's have been over for some time. The business of enlarging one's consciousness is no longer primary in people's minds. You don't hear much about it anymore.

It's still primary in contemporary American poetry. Poets who were trying to do that in their work are still very much read.

I don't think so. It is what has just passed. These things vanish as swiftly as they come. I'm not saying you won't find poets that are working in this line of expanding consciousness, for example, Robert Bly. But it is no longer a thing you hear much about. Now what you do hear a great deal about nowadays, and everybody seems to be much more conscious of, is the need for human community. This kind of talk came in after the expanding-consciousness people. People started saying we must ecologize, preserve the environment, and learn to live in a human community. This is much late 1970s talk. Of course, Wordsworth directs himself exactly to those questions.

Would it be fair to say that one led to the other? After individuals began to expand their awareness, expand their own consciousness, they realized that it was not enough. One has to live in a community and try to live harmoniously.

Yes. There's no question that people who are going to expand their consciousness by themselves are going to have to withdraw more and more from human activity and contact. I personally believe consciousness is best expanded, and the imagination is certainly best used, when it is in contact with other human beings. Wordsworth's imagination worked most vividly when he was in contact with situations outside himself.

You seem to see Wordsworth as the poet of human community, whereas others view him as mystic. How can we explain this disparity?

I don't think there is a disparity. I think both things are compatible. I very much view Wordsworth as a mystic. Now, I don't like the word "mystic." I think he's a philosophic poet. I prefer that description of Wordsworth. That does not address itself to the human community necessarily. The Wordsworth of the "spots of time" passages is a very great poet. I think that Wordsworth is a great original. Wordsworth's importance is that he is really one of the few great original thinkers.

Let me say something that I don't know if many people know. Proust is the great modern novelist who does the equivalent of Wordsworth's "spots of time" passages. *Remembrance of Things Past* is held together, finally, by these moments of perception that Marcel, the hero, has had—into an order of reality beyond that of everyday life. You do know that Proust had translated Ruskin's *Sesame and Lilies*. And Ruskin had read Wordsworth very carefully. The lines from Wordsworth's "spots of time" passages, or way of looking at nature, or looking through nature as a veil, through which you perceive an eternal power that works through man and through nature— that way of thinking descends to one of the very greatest of novelists of the twentieth century, to Proust. I don't know if anyone has traced this line of descent, but it is a very real one.

Is the influence conscious? Are Wordsworth's "spots of time" passages and that manner of perception consciously inherited by Proust, or did Wordsworth and Proust come to similar experiences?

Ruskin is the missing link. Ruskin is the bridge. Proust translates Ruskin. Ruskin is steeped in Wordsworth, as so many people in the nineteenth century were. When you ask was it conscious—no. Like many ideas one has, you get them without being able to explain exactly how.

You've said that Wordsworth's theory of composition has been misunderstood. Why?

Yes. Many misunderstand what Wordsworth meant by the origin of poetic creativity. Many people, even very intelligent men, such as T. S. Eliot, misquote Wordsworth. They say that Wordsworth believed that poetry was emotion recollected in tranquility. Wordsworth never said that. Wordsworth said that poetry takes its *origin* from emotion recollected in tranquility, which puts a completely different cast on the thing. In other words, you have an emotion which is remembered. You begin with memory. Then from the remembered emotion, which is the origin of the poem, you then begin a creative process which is right in the present. You create something that is a poem which is quite unlike mere memory or nostalgia or sentimental recollection. It's a new creation.

Then Wordsworth's analytical method makes the "spots of time" passages unique.

That's right. He picks these times when something made a very powerful impression upon him. He tries to recreate the circumstances so that he will recreate the original impression. In the process of recreating the original impression, something new begins to happen in the poem itself. The passage in *The Prelude* which describes crossing the Alps is not the same thing as the actual experience he had at the time. As he himself says in his poems, what has happened is that he has developed a philosophic mind, and that is what creates the poem.

Let me ask a related question, which goes back to an earlier one. If we have these two Wordsworths, or you made clear that it's really not two

Wordsworths but two different aspects of one integrated poet, doesn't there come a time when one has a choice as to where one puts his attention?

Can't the poet choose to develop and focus his attention on mystical experience, making a poetry out of that, or focus on human ordinary experience, compassionately, dramatically, but not with the perception of eternity and unity that a mystical poet has?

You see, for Wordsworth, the mystical power, whatever it was, worked through nature, and through men, and through men's behavior. It was visible in actions, in gestures, in moments, situations, and circumstances. It was always visible through these things. That's why he is so different from Blake. For Blake, nature is only an obstacle, an obstruction to the direct vision of God or whatever Blake would call the power.

Wordsworth needs the material world. Wordsworth is therefore very close to Oriental ways of thought, very close to the Buddhists. Nansen, the Buddhist master, says in a wonderful sentence: "Your ordinary life, that is the way." Wordsworth is very much like that. R. H. Blyth, who made collections of Buddhist *haiku*, refers to Wordsworth all the time. Now Blake wants to dispense with the physical universe. For him it's a fallen world. The fact that we're living in the flesh and that we walk around under these circumstances is an example of the fall. Wordsworth thinks that the power is dynamic and still creating and working through things. "Working through," that's his phrase for it.

I want to return to the question of the function of poetry. In your essay about Wordsworth you wrote that he was a psychologist in poetry and enlarged our sympathies. I take this to mean that you see his work as a way to refine our sensibility. He himself expressed that hope in the Preface to Lyrical Ballads. *Does this also reflect your own goals? Do you see your poems as a means to reform sensibility, the psychology of your reader?*

I don't think that I can do quite the kind of thing that Wordsworth did. I'm doing something quite different. If you take *Lyrical Ballads,* in one ballad after another he's presenting a character doing a certain action, a kind of ordinary action, sometimes a pathetic action, and showing you the real reaction of the character's mind, or his real thoughts rather than any sort of stock response you might expect. He takes an old huntsman whose ankles swell and who asks the speaker of the poem to take a hoe and cut a root that the huntsman cannot cut. So Wordworth takes the hoe, the mattock, and he cuts the root for the old man who cannot cut it for himself. Then the poet says:

> The tears into his eyes were brought
> And thanks and praise seemed to run
> So fast out of his heart, I thought
> They never would have done.
>
> —I've heard of hearts unkind, kind deeds
> With coldness still returning.

Then Wordsworth makes this remarkable statement in the closing two lines: "Alas! the gratitude of men / Hath oftener left me mourning."

It seems to me that no one in the history of poetry or literature had ever said that thing. He is an original psychologist. Now in my own life I have often felt saddened by someone's gratitude. It makes you think how sad life is for some people that such a little thing can mean so much to them. Once this has been said, it seems obvious. But Wordsworth had the habit of doing that over and over again. That's what I mean by pschology. He said to himself, "In this situation what do I really feel?" Not "Is it poetic?" "Does it sound like poetry?" No. That's what makes Wordsworth so original. Not, "Is it acceptable as poetry?" But, "I'm going to say what really happens to people's feelings." It's a very remarkable thing he does.

One of the things Wordsworth hoped for was that his poems would touch the reader, so that the reader's interaction with the community would be improved. I wonder if that's a goal you are striving for in your own work.

Well, I don't really think that my poetry will make any community at all, except at the moment that the reader is reading it. I hope he is engrossed in the poem, and that he will go through the motions I went through in creating it.

Wordsworth makes an issue in the Preface of the coarsening influence of the popular culture of his time. By that, he meant Gothic novels, obsession with the fantastic, ghost stories, and the overall cheapening of taste because of the popular press. You seem to share a similar distance or disappointment in popular culture. Is this alienation endemic to being a poet?

Yes, in the contemporary world. I don't see how a poet can possibly avoid it. Start with the most immediate thing, language. Poets use language precisely and truthfully. Language all around us is being used hysterically. It's being used for commercial purposes. It's used to lie. The poet's own tool is always being diluted, blunted.

So poets are alienated by the way language is used. How about emotional or psychological alienation?

Psychologically it is very difficult to make people pay attention to a poem, which at its center (I agree with Baudelaire) is calm. However much stress there is in the poem, there is great calm and resolution in the middle of a poem or poetry.

So there isn't the audience for poetry, because that calm which is necessary to sit down and even read a poem is lacking.

Well, you said it. People have to read. Reading itself is an act of attention. I'm not being cynical when I say only a small percentage of the U.S. population reads. Only a certain number of people really read. They haven't got the attention. They can't read a serious novel, much less a poem.

It seems to me that Wordsworth had more hope his poetry could build a community or affect positive change than what contemporary poets can hope for. Popular culture has so much overtaken life. Wordsworth's time was a period of transition. England was just moving into an industrial revolution and there was still, I would guess, a feeling of hope on his own part that his poetry could affect many readers, not just a small group or following. Whereas now, although poets might still cherish that goal for their work, realistically they acknowledge that it's next to impossible.

As I was listening to you I was disagreeing with you. I usually agree with what you just said. Listening to you I have developed another idea, which is this: Wordsworth did not really think he was going to reach thousands and thousands of readers. In Wordsworth's time, of course, most of the population did not read. But Wordsworth could be quite sure that he would reach a limited, but very powerful, influential audience of readers. For example, the kind of men and women who came out of British public schools in the nineteenth century and then went on to govern India. Quite often these were men and women who read poetry.

Darwin is an example. Darwin was tremendously influenced by Wordsworth.

Right. So the people that Wordsworth would aim at would be the readers who were very powerful, although the masses, the common soldier, the sailors, would never read anything. Now in our time, the tragedy for the American poet is that we do not have the cultured audience of influential people. The men and women who come out of American universities do not read poetry. This is what is tragic.

Also, power is so diffused today.

But you see, a doctor or a lawyer in Wordsworth's time would have been very well-read in literature. A doctor or lawyer today in America will quite often pride himself on knowing absolutely nothing about it. May I say that's not true of physicists for some reason. Physicists also are very knowledgeable about music. It's interesting.

Much is made of Wordsworth's associative abilities. How important is free association to your writing, especially as your poetry has changed over the years?

It used to be much more natural for me to freely associate. When I was a young poet, I created metaphors all the time, which is now what we're really talking about. Metaphors are associations between one thing and another. Aristotle said it was the main tool of the poet, or the main sign of a poet. For the last fifteen years I have been reducing metaphors in my work (perhaps I had to because they did not come as easily) and paying more attention to accurate description of an object or an action, in the hope that the thing itself would carry a weight of meaning.

I want to get back to process for a minute. You compared Wordsworth's description of poetic process to your own process of immersion. Can you explain this for our readers?

In order to create a dramatic narrative or to tell a story or to describe a scene in a poem, you must remember. Even if you are creating a new scene or an imaginary scene, it is built on memory, on something you have actually experienced. I throw myself back into a time when I saw something and try to relive it. I think about it until it becomes real to me, and then from that I start to make up someting that happens in that same situation. That's very difficult indeed. That's the difficult part of it.

By "immersion," I mean thinking yourself back into actual experience, and feeling and rehearsing and reliving what has occurred to you at different times of your life. It's not submersion because you are keeping your head above water, thinking and rearranging things. Submersion would be just sheer reporting, just sheer naturalism. It would not be art at all, without significance. The trick is to base something in life, something you've actually experienced or have persuaded yourself you have actually experienced.

So in "immersion" the original experience may change for you. What's happened is altered by your memory or by your poetic technique.

There is a further stage of this which is very interesting. You can actually start . . . I've actually started to tell a story and then it's failed. Then, after the passing of a year or two, I've looked back on that failed poem, and the story that I didn't tell then has become a part of my life. It's almost as real as things that really happened to me. Then I can think about it as a real thing almost and try to work from it again.

Let's switch gears for a moment. In the sixties, the war in Vietnam created moral doubts about our own culture. Culture was seen as the antagonist to genuine creative activity. Did this prompt your Wordsworthian position to conceive of poems as speculative instruments for discovering values?

What it did stimulate me to do was to move away from thinking about America as a large abstract entity, a nation. You see, I came here from the West Indies as a boy, as you know. I liked to think of America with a capital *A*, as converts do. Now in the last fifteen years, especially since the war in Vietnam, I have more or less felt that thinking about America as a large, homogenous mass is false. If you do, then you get very dismayed. You start to think about the government and all that which is dismaying.

Anyhow, I thought I would start trying to build in my books little pictures of real people rather than thinking of this abstract mass America. I would try to get to the lives of Americans.

That's a very interesting tack to take, because I think so many poets reacted violently against America, against government, with a great deal of outrage. I'm thinking of people like Allen Ginsberg and Robert Bly, who chose to either express their outrage or satirize American culture, often bitterly. You seem to have taken a different route.

I don't see myself as superior to American culture, though I have satirized aspects of it from time to time. If you think you are operating from a superior position you are ultimately not very convincing. Your poetry loses humanity and loses interest.

At what age did Wordsworth become important to you? So many who are attracted to the Romantics are first taken by Keats. He is the poet of youth. Wordsworth becomes more appealing at middle age. He has a mature vision. I'm wondering if this is your experience.

Yes, certainly. When I first read the Romatics, the greatest Romantic poem for me was Coleridge's "Ancient Mariner," and I would still not put that second to any poem ever written. I think it is one of the truly great poems of the world. I did not really love Wordsworth or think about Wordsworth very deeply until I started to teach him in my early thirties, when I taught a course at Columbia on the Romantic period.

I started to read Wordsworth in the anthology, and the more I read him, the more I read *The Prelude,* the more I started to feel this man had a great deal to say to me about being a poet and the poetic process. He's very original. He's not attractive. He doesn't attract you like Shelley or Keats when you are young, but you don't lose Wordsworth.

Do you know the poem by Matthew Arnold about the great poets who have died? Byron, Goethe, and he names them one after another. But the greatest one we cannot do without is Wordsworth. Arnold puts his finger on the quality. He says it is Wordsworth's "healing power."

Realists

July 23, 1980
Have finished *He Knew He Was Right* and begun *The Claver-ings* . . .

When one considers the novel, its special province, "life," Trollope is unbeatable. He has a broad knowledge of men and manners. Other novelists have this—Trollope's peculiar strength is his moderation.

Consider Captain Boodle's conversation with Archie in which he advises him how to go about wooing Lady Ongar. The advice is proffered in terms having to do with horses, Captain Boodle's trade: "When I've got to do with a trained mare, I always choose that she shall know that I'm there." Think what Dickens might have made of Captain Boodle! But Trollope is content to tickle our funnybone and get on with the story.

In the *Autobiography* he tells how, before beginning each day's work, he read some pages from the day before. In this way he maintained an even tone, like the rising of the sun every day.

Trollope is not Zola: blood is not shed in front of us, but lives are at stake all the same. The scene in which Harry Clavering confesses to Cecilia Burton that he has been seeing Julia Ongar, and being "false" to Cecelia's sister, is painful . . . so painful that, like Harry, we wish it were over. Harry forfeits the affection Cecelia has had for him up to now. In

---

This essay first appeared in the *Hudson Review* 34, no. 4 (Winter 1981–82).

her eyes he sees himself clearly for the first time: he is not a fine fellow, but very ordinary. This is all, yet it is everything—in a sense Harry dies.

In *The Claverings* Trollope is writing about a young man who has no character, as does Flaubert in *L'Education sentimentale*. I'm not sure but that Trollope does a better job.

July 27

Well, *The Claverings* fell apart, and it's clear why Trollope isn't ranked with the great novelists. From the moment that Harry Clavering decides to break with Julia Ongar and go back to his insipid fiancée, not because he wants to but because it is the conventionally "right" thing to do, we cease to care one way or the other. Yet Trollope goes on turning out his eight pages a day, tying up loose ends. As though it mattered!

In his autobiography Trollope attributes the comparative failure of this novel to the "weakness" of Harry Clavering, by which he seems to mean moral weakness. But the weakness of a fictional character can be interesting, even attractive. The reason for the failure of the novel is Trollope's weakness as an artist. This writer who was capable of laboring like a navvy, turning out so many pages every day, even on board ship, was also capable of avoiding a serious treatment of the subject.

To understand Harry Clavering, one would have to share his life . . . even at the risk of tedium, as Flaubert shares the life of Frédéric Moreau. That is taking the thing one has created seriously . . . the life of imagination can take you into some dreary places.

But this is at the risk of putting off your reader. It is a risk Trollope is not willing to take. So he washes his hands of Harry Clavering and lets Victorian morality dictate the rest of the novel. In the light of that morality Harry is a "weakling"—the author has abandoned his task and taken a seat in the audience. "Look at what an ass Harry Clavering is making of himself, like the ass between two bundles of hay."

This reminds me of the inconsistency in *He Knew He Was Right*. At the outset Trollope makes Emily Trevelyan obstinate, even perverse, in refusing to accede to her husband's wish and continuing to receive the visits of Colonel Osborne. It is clear that she is engaged in a struggle with her husband for power. At the end of the novel, however, it appears that the fault is all on his side, and she is the loyal wife who has been unjustly accused—a figure in a painting by Augustus Egg.

In spite of his knowledge of men and women, Trollope is willing to settle for a conventional view. The perverseness of Emily Trevelyan is sacrificed to the cliché of the dutiful, long-suffering wife. Harry Clavering does not go to bed with Julia Ongar—instead he goes back to his fiancée. Then he comes into an inheritance, an ending with which no one can quarrel . . . the *deus ex machina* of the Victorian novel.

The truth about Trollope is that he was lazy—a more serious writer would have written less. As F. R. Leavis said, the novels do not say anything to justify their length; they merely serve to kill time, "which seems to be all that even some academic critics demand of a novel."

August

The same female protagonist, at different stages in her life, appears in Jean Rhys's novels, *Quartet, After Leaving Mr. Mackenzie, Voyage in the Dark,* and *Good Morning, Midnight.* She also appears in the short stories.

We can give her a composite history by rearranging the episodes. As she has several names, for the sake of consistency let us call her X.

She grows up on an island in the West Indies, before the Great War. Her father is an Englishman—her mother, West Indian.

Her mother dies and her father marries again. The stepmother is English, the worst sort of colonizing type—she despises the natives. When X's father dies, her stepmother sends her to England to finish her schooling, then swindles her out of her inheritance.

X finds work in the chorus of a road show that plays in the provinces. She becomes familiar with dreary streets and rooms. She takes a lover and loses her virginity. The lover abandons her. X is pregnant and has to have an abortion. The lover pays for this.

X has other relationships with men. At some point in this composite history one of the men settles an amount of money upon her, to be paid regularly through a lawyer. Then the payments stop.

X is in Paris, working as a fashion model. Then it is after the war, and she is married to a Dutchman who engages in shady speculations. X acquires a fur coat that represents a certain kind of success. Then her husband is wanted by the police, and suddenly X is poor. She has a child that dies because she can't afford to have it taken care of properly.

By the time she is thirty X has begun to deteriorate. She drinks too much. She isn't too proud to accept money from men who are practically strangers. She has been evicted from hotels. She is no longer young.

There is no sentimentality in Jean Rhys's perception of X. On the contrary, at moments she treats her with a kind of gallows humor. When things are as bad as they could be, X is sure to do something to make them worse.

The key to X's character and fate is in the following passage between her and her stepmother.

> "I hate dogs," I said.
> "Well, really!" she said.
> "Well, I do," I said.
> "I don't know what'll become of you if you go on like that," Hester said. "Let me tell you that you'll have a very unhappy life if you go on like that. People won't like you. People in England will dislike you very much if you say things like that."

X will not have a happy life, because she speaks her mind—it is as simple as that.

This reckless and admirable trait makes her an outsider. Respectable people dislike her instinctively and look for ways to humiliate her and beat her down.

They don't dislike her because she is a woman or because she is poor (Jean Rhys doesn't fall into the category of a feminist or a social reformer). They dislike X and seek to humiliate her because she speaks her mind and looks it, refusing to "knuckle under." As she is a woman alone, and has no money, they are able to treat her badly and get away with it.

In a confrontation with her sister who has done the "right thing" all her life, X says, "All the people who've knuckled under—you're jealous. D'you think I don't know? You're jealous of me, jealous, jealous. Eaten up with it."

She is right—they envy her freedom of spirit. And they will punish her continually for having it.

Jean Rhys drew on her life for this fiction—her autobiography makes this clear. But she is not sentimental; she stands away from X and lets you see her weaknesses. So we can believe her when she shows the others to be contemptible. The motif, man's inhumanity to man, that rises from this fiction rings true.

If instead of writing novels and short stories at intervals, Jean Rhys had written one big, continuous novel, she might be far better known. As it is, we have only these few short novels and short stories. As Ingres once remarked, "With talent, you do what you like. With genius, you do what you can."

August 25

Many years ago, having read *César Birotteau* and *Cousin Pons*, I decided I'd had enough of Balzac—it had been a painful experience. Now, with *Lost Illusions*, I am again puzzled by the pleasure he takes in showing the triumph of the strong over the weak.

Balzac is the novelist *par excellence*. If you had to choose one novelist to represent the genus, the energy a novelist needs to have, the curiosity about human behavior, the inventiveness, it would be Balzac. He was everything that the public believes an artist to be: romantic, extravagant, obsessed. Because he believed it himself.

Balzac is inexhaustibly creative. This one novel is a world in itself, full of living characters: Lucien Rubempré, the poet who longs to be admired and who betrays everyone; who becomes remorseful and, at the first breath of fame, recovers . . . Mme. de Bargeton, the romantic woman at thirty-six, sensitive, proud, verging on the ridiculous . . . Séchard, the old miser who is also a drunkard—masterly touch!—and who is willing to ruin his own son . . . Séchard is as comical a miser as Harpagon. In any other literature do misers loom so large?

The picture of manners among the provincial aristocracy seems to have been done from the inside. And Balzac's knowledge of the paper-manufacturing business is staggering—in fact, he knows too much. A young man, having proposed marriage to the woman he loves, and been accepted, sits with her in the moonlight and delivers a lecture on papermaking. "Labor is very cheap in China, where a workman earns three halfpence a day, and this cheapness enables the Chinese to manipulate each sheet of paper separately." Et cetera. This may very well be the most ridiculous love scene in literature.

This kind of extravagance, however, comes of superabundant energy—other novelists are not capable of rising to Balzac's faults. He cannot help plunging into the details of business and legal proceedings. When one of his characters draws up an "account of expenses," Balzac gives it to you, item by item. He invests facts with a vitality they have in no other novelist. In a novel by Balzac a debt of six thousand francs is alive—it breathes, pursues its prey, and pounces.

In his passion for facts Balzac may, indeed, be closer to the urgent concerns of the nineteenth century than the innumerable novelists who wrote about love. He is the best historian of the rise of the bourgeoisie, and for this he has been praised by the Communists, from Lenin to Lukacs.

I concede that Balzac is writing history. Still, he strikes me as a kind of monster. To render the cruelties of life as energetically as Balzac does, and in such detail, is to take pleasure in them. He admires his human tigers of the counting house and Bourse.

A footnote . . . Henry James on Balzac. Speaking of Balzac's ambition, or compulsion, to write about everything, James says, "It amounts to a sort of suffered doom, since to be solicited by the world from all quarters at once, what is that for the spirit but a denial of escape? We feel his doom to be want of a private door, and that he felt it, though more obscurely, himself."

This a profound observation. But then, so many of us have a "private door," and so few can create like Balzac.

August 28

His name was Benito Pérez Galdós. He was very famous in Spain before the Great War—his play, *Electra,* was a rallying point for liberals. His historical novels were read by everyone; his realistic fiction met with some resistance but came to be regarded highly. There was agitation to obtain the Nobel prize for Galdós—committees were formed, et cetera—but he didn't get it. He died in 1920.

And I had never heard of Galdós. There's no doubt that reputations in the arts follow the flag, and Spain is no longer a great empire. On the other hand, when I was growing up in the British West Indies we read Robert Louis Stevenson. There were hundreds of English classics, some French . . . and none in German, Spanish, or Italian. I am exaggerating slightly—one had heard of *Don Quixote.*

As for the Russians . . . I suppose that one of the young men who were imported from Oxford and Cambridge to teach us might have heard of Tolstoy or Dostoevski, but if so he never passed on the word.

Now here is Galdós, and he can bear comparison with the novelists of England and France and Russia. I have only read *Miau,* his novel about an old civil servant who is out of work and seeking reemployment . . . but how many books does one have to read before one decides that a writer is "great"? One great book is enough to settle a man's claim, in my opinion.

Galdós has the quality all great novelists share—he is interested in everyone. A character has only to appear for a minute, and he's alive. There are no supernumerary characters—everyone has a life, and it's important. *Miau* gives off what Henry James described as "that vague hum, that indefinable echo of the whole multitudinous life of man, which is the real sign of a great work of fiction."

The novel centers on two people: the old man, Villaamil, who grows wilder and wilder as other, less deserving men are given positions or receive promotions while he, with all his years of loyal, honest service to the State, and his brilliant plan for instituting an income tax, is left out in the cold; and his grandchild, Luis, who is in the way of becoming a saint. Luis has visions of God and converses with him. It is very difficult to get his grandfather a job, God tells Luis. He tells people what to do, but they don't listen.

And if Luis doesn't do his homework, how can his grandfather find a position? Luis hasn't been studying; in his geography lesson he misplaced a town and a river. What's the use of making a world, if people are going to throw things around?

Besides Luis there are a family of "Miaus," his grandmother and his aunts, who have been given this nickname because they look like cats. There is Luis's father, who is wicked for the love of it. And a wonderful dog named Canelo.

The visions of Luis are not dreams or hallucinations—Galdós makes this quite clear, though you'd have to read the novel to see how. The realism of Galdós is "psychological"—everything is related to the workings of the minds of his characters, not conjured out of thin air. The God whom little Luis sees is as believable as the human characters, because Luis sees him.

By the end of the story the demarcation between "real life" and the life of ideas has vanished. Galdós shows that practically anything can be accomplished within the mode of realism—you can be as imaginative as you like, as well as "true to life."

Critics like to say that the term "realism" has no meaning. For what is the "real"? It is what you think—"thinking makes it so." They prefer to discuss realism as a literary movement, the leader of which was Champfleury, who may have been a realist but was certainly trivial.

But though you may not be able to define a thing exactly, it may exist nonetheless. Realism is a definite way of looking at things, and a way of writing, recognizably different from other kinds.

The realist aims to create an illusion of life. Fantastic images, supernatural events, and dogmatic ideas have no place in such writing unless they are presented as happening in the minds of the characters.

The realist attempts at all times to present a picture of life that is recognizably true.

Of course one can think of anything and assert it is true, but this is not useful. Truth is that which is true to our experience. In the words of William James, "True ideas are those that we can assimilate, validate, corroborate, and verify. False ideas are those we can not . . .

"The truth of an idea is not a stagnant property inherent in it. Truth *happens* to an idea. It *becomes* true, is *made* true by events . . .

". . . truth [is] something essentially bound up with the way in which one moment in our experience may lead us towards other moments which it will be worth while to have been led to."

The Santa Claus of Loneliness

God is dead, said Nietzsche. Abandoned by God, philosophers and poets turned to expressing their psyches. Freud invented psychoanalysis, and Rainer Maria Rilke wrote poems about the Inner Life.

Literary history makes for these scenarios; authors are seen as embodying ideas and setting out to express their times. But biography suggests that it happens the other way round: the life we have determines the ideas by which we live. Rilke is a case in point. He was born into one of those socially aspiring and ineffectual bourgeois families that have provided the substance of a hundred plays and novels. Prague, where he grew up, Rilke described as a "miserable city of subordinate existences." His father had declined from an army officer to a petty clerk for the railroad. Rilke's mother was by turns religious and ambitious to get on in society. Her infant daughter died, so that when Rilke was a small child she dressed him as a girl and called him "Miss." Like Proust, Rilke never knew that domestic happiness toward which the middle class directed its energy and by which it justified the punishments inflicted on its members. Rilke's early sorrows forced him into a premature retirement—he may be said to have

---

This review of *The Selected Poetry of Rainer Maria Rilke,* edited and translated by Stephen Mitchell; and *The Roses and The Windows, The Astonishment of Origins, Orchards* by Rainer Maria Rilke, translated by A. Poulin, Jr., appeared in the *Washington Post Book World,* December 5, 1982.

never truly lived. His life went into his poetry, where it vibrated with energy.

Much of his life was spent waiting for visitations of the power that enabled him to write. He paid little attention to the world, had none of the fascination with men and women that one finds in Homer and Chaucer, even in Baudelaire. Rilke thought about "things"—the "Santa Claus of loneliness," Auden calls him. To Rilke things were masks through which another world was striving to be seen and heard. Baudelaire said it long ago: we walk through a forest of symbols that watch us with knowing eyes. Our part is to enter into things and meet the other world halfway. Rilke wrote, "Perhaps we are *here*, in order to say: house / bridge, fountain, gate, pitcher, fruit-tree, window."

Our deprivations, the powers we do not have, are seen as existing in the antiworld—absences here become presences there. Rilke calls them angels, and calls upon them to listen to his poems, the voice that expresses things of this world. But he does not know if they are listening: "Who, if I cried, would hear me among the angelic orders?" And if an angel did respond, would the poet be able to withstand contact with the angel's stronger existence? The end to which the poet strives is annihilation of the poet. And so he holds back, repressing the "call-note." For years Rilke held back until at Duino the angel came flooding in.

"Who, if I cried, would hear me among the angelic orders?" This trumpet call launches the *Duino Elegies*. The *Elegies*, together with *Sonnets to Orpheus*, which were written directly afterwards, are Rilke's most astonishing poetry—it makes other poetry seem earthbound in comparison. I have quoted the line in the 1939 translation by J. B. Leishman and Stephen Spender, the only translation available at the time. One's first reading of a poem, like first love, leaves an ineffaceable impression, and though I have been told by people expert in German that the Leishman-Spender version is too smooth, even soft, I still keep hearing it.

Rilke wrote: "Wer, wenn ich schriee, horte mich denn aus

der Engel / Ordnungen?" Stephen Mitchell has given us the German text on facing pages, as every translator of poetry should. He translates the lines as follows: "Who, if I cried out, would hear me among the angels' / hierarchies?" The Leishman-Spender "orders" is surely closer than "hierarchies" to the sound of "ordnungen." I do not find anything particularly attractive about "hierarchies"—on the contrary, it seems professorial. Perhaps translators do not always use the most suitable words—they put aside the most suitable words because they have been used by other translators, and choose other words.

I own three previous translations of the *Duino Elegies:* the Leishman-Spender translation; a translation by Stephen Garmey and Jay Wilson, published in 1972; and a translation by A. Poulin Jr., published in 1977. In order to compare Mitchell's translation with these other, older versions, I chose his translation of a passage by Rilke that is, for me, the best thing he ever said:

> Perhaps we are *here* in order to say: house,
> bridge, fountain, gate, pitcher, fruit-tree, window—
> at most; column, tower. . . . But to *say* them, you must understand,
> oh to say them *more* intensely than the Things themselves
> ever dreamed of existing.

There is trouble here with the understanding. One has to search to find the connection between "dreamed of existing" and "to say . . . more intensely." And when one has found it, the syntax is slightly askew—certainly one has to force it into sense. A second fault is the sound of the lines. They are prosaic. The German is as follows:

> aber zu *sagen,* verstehs,
> oh zu sagen *so,* wie selber die Dinge niemals
> innig meinten zu sein.

My German exists in a Rilkean antiworld; still, I can make this out, and it is far more poetic than the translation. The German words are short and resonant. The translator's "ever dreamed of existing" makes the passage topple over heavily at the end.

Leishman and Spender translated these lines:

> but for saying, remember,
> oh, for such saying as never the things themselves
> hoped so intensely to be.

The meaning here is clearer than in the Mitchell version, but not much, and "to be . . . such saying" is not idiomatic. As for style, it is breathless, a big gushy.

Stephen Garmey and Jay Wilson wrote:

> but to say them, understand me,
> *so* to say them as the things within themselves never
> thought to be.

This pushes the fault of the Leishman-Spender translation one step further, so that the passage doesn't make sense: "to be" requires an object, and "to say them" is not it.

Turning to A. Poulin Jr.:

> but to say them, remember,
> oh, to say them in a way that the things themselves
> never dreamed of existing so intensely.

For clarity I would give this first place. We can see what it is that things never dreamed of: "a way," and that they never dreamed it could exist so intensely. The lines, however, are no closer to the poetic sounds of the original than Mitchell's version.

Taking one thing with another, I prefer the translations by Mitchell and Poulin. The lines I chose to compare are difficult—in other places Mitchell conveys Rilke's meaning clearly. As for the sound of his translations, it would be ill-natured to find fault with him for failing to sound as interesting in English as Rilke does in German. I would rather have his accurate translations than the kind in which the translator writes his own poetry at the expense of the author.

Mitchell has selected from the entire range of Rilke's poetry: from *The Book of Hours, The Book of Pictures, New Poems, Requiem, Uncollected Poems,* and *The Sonnets to Orpheus,* as well as the *Duino Elegies.* There is a selection from the prose *Notebooks of Malte Laurids Brigge.* I don't know of any other selection of Rilke's writing that is so representative, and it is portable, convenient to take with you. The *Cornet* is not represented, nor Rilke's *Letters to a Young Poet,* but I suppose you can't have everything in one easy volume.

Robert Hass has a fairly long introduction to Mitchell's selection of Rilke's poetry. I rather dislike Hass's chatty touches: telling us how, in Paris, he went looking for a café where Rilke had breakfast, and about a friend named Fred who was hungry "and could not have cared less where Rilke ate breakfast." Fred showed good sense: information about such matters may have some bearing on the life of a hip poet, the kind who hangs out, but it can tell us nothing about Rilke, whose life, in his own eyes, was of no importance, the poetry everything. Hass is much better when he explains that poetry, and very good indeed when he tells us how the *Elegies* were put together and describes their effect on the readers: "The author of these poems is everywhere. Really, they are the nearest thing in the writing of the twentieth century to the flight of birds. They dive, soar, swoop, belly up, loop over. . . . The subject is the volatility of emotion."

Between February 1922 when he completed the *Duino Elegies* and *Sonnets to Orpheus* and December 1926 when he died, Rilke wrote nearly four hundred poems in French. In a poem titled "Verger" he says that he wrote in French in order to use the word "verger" (orchard). This is the kind of witticism Oscar Wilde might have made, but though it is witty it may be true: Rilke may have written in French because he liked the sound of the words.

His French poems sound like Verlaine. They are lighter in tone than his poems in German. The content also seems lighter, perhaps because it is familiar: we have known these angels, loaves of bread, and windows. But Rilke is always capable of astonishing, as in these lines from *The Astonishment of Origins.*

The translation is again by Poulin, who translated the *Duino Elegies* and has also translated *The Sonnets to Orpheus.*

> Look at a child's index and thumb—
> so gentle a vise,
> even bread is astonished.

And these lines from *Orchards:* "None of us advances / but towards a silent god." Had anyone thought of this before? Or said it so memorably?

These poems, however, must have seemed old-fashioned in Paris of the twenties. Symbolist poetry was old hat. The Futurists had heaped ridicule upon Symbolism—the poetry of the future would speak of racing cars, airplanes, and battleships. Dadaists turned all writing into a joke, and Surrealists were inventing images, not exploring an inner world. A German poet, Walter Mehring, who read poems in cabarets, told me that one day, strolling with Rilke in Paris, he told Rilke that his poems in French were awful. But everything passes, and Rilke's poems are no more old-fashioned now than the writings of the Futurists, Dadaists, and Surrealists. They do strike me, however, as delicate. I miss the ruggedness of Rilke's poems in German, the cragginess of his style and his formidable subjects. In German Rilke may write about a drunkard, a blind man, or a panther. In French he writes a great deal about roses.

Poulin has translated the French poems in four volumes, and there is another still to come. He is a deft translator, with sympathy for Rilke's ideas and a nice sense of the rhythm of lines. I doubt that anyone could have done the job better, and until now, it appears, no one thought of doing it.

The books, by the Graywolf Press, are attractively bound and printed. They fit in the pocket—just the thing to read at a play or concert during the intermissions.

William Carlos Williams

The poetry of William Carlos Williams is hardly known in Australia, yet of all American poets who have written in this century he is the most influential—not among critics, for many have never accepted him—but among young poets and readers of poetry. As Williams is unknown by the general reader, I shall lay out for you some of the general facts of his life before I discuss his ideas and his writing.

He was born in Rutherford, New Jersey, in 1883 of an English father and a Puerto Rican mother. Unlike Pound and Eliot who came of a long line of American ancestors, Williams felt he was an outsider and that he had to affirm his citizenship. All his life he would be preoccupied with what it meant to be an American and all his life he would be in revolt against the English culture to which his father was attached. Williams's father, though he had lived in America, never became an American citizen but remained British.

The family traveled to Europe when Williams was a boy. He attended schools in Switzerland and in France, but completed his high school education at Horace Mann, in New York. One day, while training for track he strained his heart and was never again able to take part in athletics. Then he

---

I gave this talk at Macquarie University, Sydney, Australia, in May 1979, at a conference on the relationship between Australian and American poetry. It was published in *The American Model: Influence and Independence in Australian Poetry*, edited by Joan Kirkby (Sydney: Hale and Iremonger, 1982).

went to the University of Pennsylvania where he studied medicine. There he met the poets Ezra Pound and Hilda Doolittle.

Though Williams had begun to write poetry, he did not think he could make a living that way and he liked to be with people, he liked the human contact. He had written a long epic poem imitative of Keats's "Endymion," and he was keeping a notebook in which he wrote in the manner of Whitman. But when he showed the Keats imitation to a professor of English the professor told him he might be a poet in about twenty years. That was too long to wait. For the sake of security and to be sure that any writing he did would be free of commercial pressure he became a doctor.

Williams remained a doctor all his life and, except for brief excursions to Europe, lived all his life in Rutherford where he had been born. He married a woman named Florence Hermann in 1912 and remained married to her all his life. They had two sons, one of whom became a doctor, the other a businessman.

Williams's first book of poems was privately printed in 1913; from that time on he came in contact with other poets and for the rest of his life he would have two careers: one at his office or the hospital, the other in New York where he met poets and painters—he was a friend of the painters Sheeler and Demuth with whose paintings his work has clear affinities. Williams published books of poems throughout the 1920s. In the 1930s he turned increasingly to writing prose, that is, novels and short stories. He was not, however, a popular writer. In fact, it was not until the 1950s that he became generally recognized as an important American poet. He was then adopted as an ancestor by Allen Ginsberg and the Beat poets, though he repudiated the connection.

In 1951 Williams suffered a stroke and retired from medical practice. His poems were republished in collected editions and in 1958 he brought his long poem *Paterson* to a conclusion; he wrote new poems which people said were his best. An autobiography, a collection of letters, a collection of plays, two collections of reminiscences—one recognizes the signs of a career drawing to a close. Williams died in Rutherford on March 4, 1963.

It is not a dramatic life. Williams is the antithesis of a poet such as Dylan Thomas whose life and personality compete for interest with his art. Williams was domestic; though he had affairs with other women, he held on to his marriage. He practiced medicine conscientiously though he frequently complained that it kept him away from writing. He was not reconciled to his life but it was preferable to any alternative. He was critical, for example, of Pound and Eliot who had uprooted themselves and gone to Europe. Speaking of such people, Williams says, "In every case, they have forgotten or not known that the experience of native local contacts which they take with them is the only thing that can give that differentiated quality of presentation to their work which first enriches their new sphere and then later alone might carry them far as creative artists in the continental hurly-burly. Pound ran to Europe in a hurry; it is understandable; but he had not sufficient ground to stand on for more than perhaps two years, he stayed fifteen. . . ."

In the 1920s, when Williams by his own choice found himself living in Rutherford while Pound and Eliot were enjoying the cultural flesh-pots of London or Paris or Rapallo, he developed a theory of localism. He was not the only one to do so: John Dewey, in an essay in the *Dial,* had said that the American novel was failing because it lacked a structure of manners and that manners were a product of the interaction of characters and social environment. Hermann Keyserling, also writing in the 1920s, attributed the lack of soul in America to the immigrants' having cut themselves off from their roots. However, said Keyserling, the pressure on immigrants to standardize their minds would turn them into localists; this was absolutely necessary for the development of an indigenous culture. "Culture," said Keyserling, "is always a daughter of spirit, married to earth."

It is not easy to understand what locality meant to Williams, and many of his admirers have gone wrong on this point. Williams did not mean that you had to write about your own particular Rutherford and nothing else. He was not so provincial. It must be admitted, however, that some of his remarks would lead you to think so, for Williams was, at times, a hasty writer, especially when he was writing prose. But when he became aware that this narrow construction might be put upon his words he repudiated it decisively. "I'm no more sentimental about America," he wrote to Pound, "than Li Po was about China. I know as well as you do that there's nothing sacred about any land but I also know that there's no taboo effective against any land."

It wasn't a geographical location that he was after, but location in experience, the experience of the writer. The movement is from the particular to the general, as Williams writes at the beginning of *Paterson:* "To make a start out of particulars and make them general." Williams wanted to arrive at general meanings, perhaps even a universal meaning, but to do so he must begin from where he was, not from where some Englishman or Frenchman had stood three hundred years ago. What kind of universal would it be if, when you got there, you found your own particular experiences missing? This is the crux of his quarrel with Eliot; all his life Williams felt that he was opposing Eliot. His remarks about *The Waste Land* are well known: how, just as things were beginning to move in American poetry, when Americans were finding a language for their poetry, Eliot's *Waste Land* exploded and wiped out their world. Eliot had sent American poetry back to the classroom. It was embittering to Williams personally to see the triumph that Eliot had in his generation. Eliot carried American readers off with him to the poetry of Europe, and then into the Anglican Church. Williams felt that but for Eliot the success would have gone to the kind of poetry based in experience, the poetry of an American language, that he himself was writing.

Perhaps it was because Eliot's success made him believe that his own poetry had failed that Williams, in the 1930s, gave most of his energy to writing prose. The poems he did write during those years are not happy. Williams said that he was using words as paint, and this is all very well, we can see the point he was trying to make, but one cannot help feeling, that after a brave and free beginning, the Williams of the 1930s is rather dry. The poem, he said, was "an object," and out of this was born the Objectivist school of Zukofsky, Oppen, and other poets of the 1930s. Words would be used for their inherent properties as sounds and movements, for anything but the general ideas they might convey. General ideas would be left to Eliot and his acolytes.

It is interesting to compare the two big volumes of Williams's poems, the *Collected Earlier Poems* and the *Collected Later Poems*. I should point out, however, that the *Collected Later Poems* does not contain Williams's last poems, the poems of *Desert Music, Journey to Love,* and *Pictures from Brueghel*. The *Collected Earlier Poems* is full of life observed with feeling; the *Collected Later Poems* too often read like academic exercises, the academy being one that Williams has imposed on himself with his ambition to use words only as paint. Here is an early poem by Williams:

This Is Just to Say

I have eaten
the plums
that were in
the icebox

and which
you were probably
saving
for breakfast

Forgive me
they were delicious
so sweet
and so cold

This poem is a good test for readers of poetry. I've seen it happen again and again: students who are particularly proud of their knowledge of English poetry will reject the poem by Williams immediately,—"Why, that's not poetry, anyone could do that." The answer, of course, would be to ask them to try.

Here is Williams's own comment on the poem: "It's curious how a thing of this sort which is really just a passing gesture actually took place just as it says here. My wife being out, I left a note for her just that way and she replied very beautifully. Unfortunately, I've lost it. I think what she wrote was quite as good as this—a little more complex, but quite as good. Perhaps the virtue of this is its simplicity."

The interviewer asked Williams what it was about "This Is Just to Say" that made it a poem. "In the first place," Williams replied, "it was metrically regular." The interviewer remarked that the poem went against the preconceived idea of poetry because it was the kind of thing almost anybody might say. "Yes," Williams said, "because no one believes that poetry can exist in his own life."

Surely this is the secret of Williams—he shows us that poetry can exist in our own lives. This is why he has been so great an influence upon young Americans; he has reclaimed their lives, however seemingly dull they may be, for poetry. He is like Chekhov and like Wordsworth, writers who concentrate on the ordinary objects about them, who charge ordinary life with excitement. Do you know the poem Matthew Arnold wrote when Wordsworth died? He said that within recent memory several great poets had died, Goethe and Byron among them, but none would be missed so much as Wordsworth, for Wordsworth had been a healing power. Others had been astonishing, had amazed the public, but Wordsworth had enabled them to feel again. This is what Williams in his early poems was able to do. As I have said, in the work of the middle period from the beginning of the 1930s to the 1940s—a period in Williams's career that coincides interestingly with the Depression—he turned to prose and in his poems seemed bound and constricted by a theory of impersonal creation. The poems he then produced seemed lacking in *affect*. There is a kind of Puritan perversity in Williams's insistence during this period on thinking of poems as objects, words as paint. Take the following poem for example, titled "Christmas 1950"; I think it's a fair choice as Williams chose it to end the later poems with:

The stores
guarded
by the lynx-eyed
dragon

money
humbly
offer their
flowers.

Kalenchios.
Spanish?
No
they originated

in Germany.
They
bloom so
long!

They're
very easy
to take care of
too

In spring
you
can put them
out

side
and they'll
thrive
there also.

Now a poet could learn something from this poem about line-breaks, but it is not an engaging piece of work. There's no *affect* in it, it comes off the top of the head.

The first book of *Paterson* was published in 1946. At several points in his writing of *Paterson* Williams expressed doubts as to what he was doing, whether it were a poem at all or a failure. I don't intend to explore the question here, but for devotees of William Carlos Williams, which Williams himself never was, *Paterson* is a hugely successful epic poem, an exploration of American language, the portrait of a city or a man. There is as much confusion in the critics' minds as to what *Paterson* is about as there was in Williams's. I'm quite certain that *Paterson* is not a successful poem as a whole; there are stretches of very good writing in it but Williams commits the error of following life. Going against his own theory of poetry, he insists on following historical fact; he prints tables of statistics and tells us many things, but never why we should be interested in this particular part of the earth's surface. Williams himself once remarked on the fatuity of Shakespeare's line about art, in which art is described as "holding a mirror up to Nature." Williams pointed out that the job of the artist is not to hold a mirror up to nature, which would be redundant—it is to learn from nature how to be creative. Nature teaches us to be ourselves; the thing created in art is different from the thing created in nature. But in *Paterson* Williams relapsed into mere naturalism. Perhaps it was the influence of the good film documentaries that were made in the thirties, or his own work on a WPA writers' project in which he studied the history of the region. Whatever the reason, he produced a poem that meanders to no point, with good stretches, as I've said, but no convincing structure. Williams's devotees have said that the very lack of structure is what is great about *Paterson*. They would like to make Williams one of the artists of chance, being to poetry what John Cage is to music. But Williams disliked chance; his whole life as man and artist was an attempt to give structure to experience. Beginning with particulars does not mean surrendering to them but transforming them into a significant shape.

Or suppose we read *Paterson* just for its language; one can indeed find passages in it that show Williams's fine ear for speech, the rhythm of American phrases. But writing that has nothing to recommend it but a style cannot be important. Even Wordsworth in *The Prelude* had more to do than this; he was describing the growth of a poet's mind. If *Paterson* is about a search for a language of poetry then it is like a snake swallowing its own tail. It is too concerned with itself to be able to move or to move us.

This is the place to say that, on this point of language, most people's idea of Williams is wrong. It is commonly said that Williams wrote as he talked or as other people talked. Allen Ginsberg tells how he went to hear Williams read his poems at the Museum of Modern Art, and when Williams read his poem "The Clouds" he left the last sentence unfinished, just trailed off the way people do when they are speaking. This, says Ginsberg, was a revelation to him. It completely destroyed his world of academic bullshit. Williams, says Ginsberg, wrote the way that he talked, that was the secret of his style. I remember that when I first read this description by Ginsberg I accepted it automatically; it explained the revolution in American poetry in the late 1950s, a revolution led by Ginsberg himself. The new poets, that is, the Beats, were writing just as they talked, there was no more division between their lives and their art. This may be true of Ginsberg, but looking at Williams's poems I see now that it is obviously not true of Williams. Here are the lines Ginsberg heard Williams read at the Museum:

> The clouds remain
> —the disordered heavens, ragged, ripped by winds
> or dormant, a calligraphy of scaly dragons and bright moths
> of straining thought, bulbous or smooth,
> ornate, the flesh itself (in which
> the poet foretells his own death); convoluted, lunging upon
> a pismire, a conflagration, a . . . .

The sentence is unfinished but is this the language of speech? Neither Williams nor anyone else used words like these in conversation. What Williams's poetry consists of is a selection of language, the language, if you like, that is used by men. In any case, it is definitely a selection. Williams's tone is that of a man thinking; his thoughts may incorporate phrases and fragments of conversation, but to say that Williams wrote as he talked is a misrepresentation and accounts for the dreary disjunctive writing that has been committed in the name of Williams since the early 1960s. Williams himself repudiated poets who wrote just as they talked: "Their trouble," he said, "was an inability to make themselves think."

The energy with which Williams returned to poetry in his later years may be attributable to the stroke. He was disabled and growing old; it was now or never, and he wrote. We may speculate about his life but there is no need to speculate about the nature of the poetry. It was the fruit of a long life of artistic self-discipline. The tools were there and all that was necessary was to get that incubus *Paterson* out of the way. Writing poetry according to a plan was the antithesis of Williams's idea of poetry. With the failure of *Paterson* he was free to write as he pleased. In these last poems there was a regeneration; the work is permeated with the feeling that had been present in Williams's early poems, but only in flashes, and dispersed in the prose. This feeling takes it origin from his sympathy with the common man and this, it may be apposite to say here, is what Williams has in common with Whitman, not the writing of free verse or any other kind of technique. Williams, I'm sorry to say, did not appreciate Whitman as a writer of verse. He thought that Whitman's writing was disordered and diffuse, without art. Than which Williams could not have been more mistaken, as I'm sure that those of you who listened to Galway Kinnell speaking yesterday on Whitman will agree.

Williams's clearest statement of what he owed as a poet to his belief in, or instinctive liking for, the common man is to be found in an essay he wrote called "The Basis of Faith in Art." It was first published in 1954 among his selected essays. "I go back to the people," he says. "They are the origin of every bit of life that can possibly inhabit any structure, house, poem or novel of conceivable human interest. It doesn't precisely come out of the tops of their heads like flowers but they represent, in themselves, the structure which art . . . Put it this way: If we don't cling to the warmth which breathes into a house or a poem alike from human need . . . the whole matter has nothing to hold it together and becomes structurally weak so that it falls to pieces."

Does this strike us as a vague prescription for writing lines of verse? I noticed a curious thing yesterday when Galway Kinnell was discussing Whitman's writing of verse, that is, his lines. He (Galway) spent most of his time discussing Whitman's quality of feeling. At one point, I recall, he himself remarked on this and proceeded to link it up saying that it was Whitman's feeling that determined how he wrote his line. This, of course, is true and the same is true of Williams. To discuss the skill with which *Pictures from Brueghel* is written is to discuss the feeling that goes into the lines and makes them move in particular ways. It is ultimately to come down to the source of Williams's feelings, his contact with men and women and his faith in democracy and America. There was nothing naive, however, about Williams's sympathies; he was a doctor and saw life in all its ugliness. But he saw it also in its passion and natural beauty.

I have said that his language is that of a man thinking. I would add that the rhythms and line-breaks are those of a man feeling. It is his urgency, his reaching out to others, that makes his lines move as they do. The American measure that he was looking for consisted of his feeling of urgency moving in short lines, the line dividing usually into three parts. He called each part a variable foot, and this has been argued over, but no matter what he called it, each division had a unity of syllables that at the moment he felt. I have said Williams's vocabulary and tone are not those of common speech but of meditation. It is equally true that the measure of Williams's lines is not that of speech but of feeling, the feelings of a certain kind of man, eager to impart his thought—almost nervous about it, in fact. "Forget all rules," he said, "forget all restrictions, write for the pleasure of it. There's a primitive profundity of the personality that must be touched, but," he hastened to add, "once the writing is on paper it becomes an object. It has entered now a new field, that of intelligence."

In *Pictures from Brueghel* we are aware that the personality of Williams has been released at last and, at the same time, the poems have the shape and solidity of objects. Consider the explosion of feeling in this poem, "Iris":

> a burst of iris so that
> come down for
> breakfast
>
> we searched through the
> rooms for
> that
>
> sweetest odor and at
> first could not
> find its
>
> source then a blue as
> of the sea
> struck
>
> startling us from among
> those trumpeting
> petals

Or consider the following passage which accomplishes a more difficult thing, wringing poetry out of unbeautiful, intractable matter. "The thing," said Williams, "that stands eternally in the way of really good writing is always one: the virtual impossibility of lifting to the imagination those things which lie under the direct scrutiny of the senses, close to the nose."

In the lines I am about to read Williams accomplishes the seemingly impossible, making the full sweep from the kind of life we see around us to the life of art, bringing life over into art. The thing that appeals about this kind of writing is that there is no limit to the material. You may run out of nightingales and Grecian urns but you cannot run out of life. But it is not the material that makes it poetry, rather the method, and this comes of a disposition of the heart:

Once at night
waiting at a station
with a friend
a fast freight
thundered through
kicking up the dust.
My friend,
a distinguished artist,
turned with me
to protect his eyes:
That's what we'd all like to be, Bill,
he said. I smiled
knowing how deeply
he meant it. I saw another man
yesterday
in the subway.
I was on my way uptown
to a meeting.
He kept looking at me
and I at him:
He had a worn knobbed stick
between his knees
suitable
to keep off dogs,
a man of perhaps forty.
He wore a beard
parted in the middle,
a black beard,
and a hat,
a brown felt hat
lighter than
his skin. His eyes,
which were intelligent,
were wide open
but evasive, mild.
I was frankly curious
and looked at him
closely. He was slight of build
but robust enough
had on

a double-breasted black coat
                and a vest
                                which showed at the neck
the edge of a heavy and very dirty
                undershirt.
                                His trousers
were striped
                and a lively
                                reddish brown. His shoes
which were good
                if somewhat worn
                                had been recently polished
His brown socks
                were about his ankles.
                                In his breast pocket
he carried
                a gold fountain pen
                                and a mechanical
pencil. For some reason
                which I could not fathom
                                I was unable
to keep my eyes off him.
                A worn leather zipper case
                                bulging with its contents
lay between his ankles
                on the floor.
                                Then I remembered:
When my father was a young man—
                it came to me
                                from an old photograph—
he wore such a beard.
                This man
                                reminds me of my father.
I am looking
                into my father's
                                face!

To Celebrate Williams

To celebrate is not to criticize, so I won't express my reservations about some of Williams's writings and opinions. In keeping with the occasion I shall confine my remarks to those aspects of his work and life that I find most appealing.

In the first place Williams tells us to look around and make poetry out of the things we see and hear every day, in language that can be understood. This is radically different from what some conceive to be the aim of poetry—that it should take us away from the familiar into a fantastic situation, and that it must be written in an affected style. Williams did not equivocate: "contact with experience," he said, "is essential to good writing." One would think that the battle for Williams's kind of writing had been won at the beginning of the nineteenth century when Wordsworth wrote, and won for Americans half a century later when Whitman published *Leaves of Grass*, but this particular battle has been won and lost many times, and at present, with the writing of some of our poets, it is being lost again. The critics are helping to lose it—they

"To Celebrate Williams" was written to be read at a "Centennial Tribute to William Carlos Williams" held by the Modern Language Association in New York City on December 29, 1983. One of the previous speakers denounced the literary establishment in sweeping terms. My own remarks on the subject would have been superfluous. . . . I did not give my talk but read three poems instead. The talk was published in the *Pacific Review* 2 (Spring 1984).

have very little understanding of the kind of poetry that addresses itself to our common life. For them poetry consists of words alone, and the best poet is the one who can contort a subject until it is no longer recognizable.

The second thing we can learn from Williams is the pleasure of finding new forms for new experiences. He spoke of writing poetry "with the bare hands," and this is the impression his poems make—they have been wrested out of the material, sometimes against the grain. One never has the feeling of language being poured into a mould to set.

Williams wrote in a rhythm that was natural to him. He called it the "variable foot" and claimed that it was an American measure. Whatever it is called, Williams's rhythm made for short lines with irregular stresses. The stresses are irregular because he is uttering phrases as a whole rather than having a Procrustes bed of iambs or anapests and fitting the phrase to the frame. Williams's system gives an effect of spontaneity and naturalness when it works, and of prosiness when it doesn't. It can give the effect Wordsworth wanted, of "a man speaking to men." The old poetry of regular feet and lines and stanzas cannot do that, in the twentieth century.

The third thing Williams teaches is how to stand up for what one believes to be the way of poetry, though no one else seems to believe in it. Williams spoke his mind—he did not court fame. I find this entirely admirable, for there is nothing more destructive of truth and poetry than running after fame.

I do not think that Williams ever belonged to an institute or academy. If someone is going to tell me that Williams was elected to an Institute of Letters or Academy of Poets, it must have been when he was very old and rather grateful for any attention shown to him. But for most of his life, isolated in Rutherford, Williams was ignored or treated with condescension by people who were his inferiors as poets and critics of poetry. As he didn't want anything from them he had the satisfaction of writing as he liked and saying what he pleased. And this is no small recompense. As Remy de Gourmont observed, "Speaking his mind frankly is the writer's one pleasure."

It gives me some pleasure to have done so, and I envy Williams his long experience of the feeling. I would advise younger poets to follow his example—it is the only way for a poet to go.

The Down-to-Earth and the
Acrobatic

The gulf is widening in American verse between poetry that
speaks from experience and makes it appeal through sen-
suous images, narrative, and drama, and poetry that is highly
mannered, aiming to derive pleasure from words alone. The
new books I am about to discuss show the contrast clearly.
They are all first books—John Bensko's has been published in
the Yale Series of Younger Poets, and Jared Carter's has been
given the Walt Whitman Award for 1980 by the Academy of
American Poets.

John Bensko's *Green Soldiers* opens with imaginary scenes
and incidents: the poet García Lorca and a one-legged school-
teacher are shot; a "Young Woman at Amiens: 1914" watches
her friend march off to the Great War. The object of inventing history in this way is to make us feel it as present. Like his
"Veteran of the Great War" the poet ". . . calls together the
neighborhood children / and tells them stories in which every
day / is today." Words create history—words, therefore, may
be history.

The second half of *Green Soldiers* speaks to a later generation and the setting is domestic—instead of the Western

This review of John Bensko's *Green Soldiers*, J. D. McClatchy's *Scenes
from Another Life,* Douglas Crase's *The Revisionist,* and Jared Carter's
Work, for the Night Is Coming appeared in the *Washington Post Book
World,* June 7, 1981.

Front, a house and back yard. It begins innocently enough with:

> Lemon peels, freshly ground ginger
> in a pile on the table, all the bright faces
> washed and ready for eating.

But we fall out of this Eden—"We learn," says the narrator, "to be good / at being guilty," and the guilt grows by leaps and bounds. In "The Pet Cat" the tale is of a cat that has eaten a canary and the retribution visited upon the cat. In this house and yard an Aeschylean tragedy develops, involving the child and his mother. Clytemnestra, Orestes, and the Furies are in the yard, watched by a chorus of toads, ants, and bees. The child moves into a universe of disembodied hands and manic behavior. The only solution appears to be to meditate and imagine.

> So the love and the meditation
> go on, turning a white sheet and a girl
> into a night-blooming cactus.

This is very bright, a brilliant book. John Bensko should go far.

J. D. McClatchy is also concerned to affirm the reality of imagination, as the title of his book, *Scenes from Another Life,* indicates. However, there is a vast difference between the two poets. Bensko writes transparent language and relies on images for intensity; the words, to use Whitman's description, don't stand like curtains between the reader and what is being presented. McClatchy on the other hand writes in a formal style that draws attention to itself. There is a marked subordination of meaning, or any drama of feeling or idea, to the form of expression. At times he echoes W. H. Auden—it is certainly the manner of Auden we hear in "A Capriccio of Roman Ruins and Sculpture with Figures," and in these lines from "The Tears of the Pilgrims":

Driving back across the border
After a cheap dinner in Spain,
The startling burst of bonfires—
Some in tenement courtyards,
But most in parking lots
Where anyone's car and orange crates
Burnt up and up into votive sparks—
Made us simultaneously afraid
And playful, as if (but by that time
Local friends in the backseat
Had explained tonight was St. John's Eve)
We too could have stopped to circle
Those shooting flames all night long.

Richard Howard, who wrote the introduction, says that the strength of McClatchy's poems is in their "attending" to both "the merely lived life, experience, which means death, and, on the other side, to the splendors of the life imagined, vision, which means—for him, at least—love." But for this reader the poems did not measure up to the praise: the experiences rendered by McClatchy are a bit tame, the splendors tend to be touristic. I am surprised to see a poet writing in 1980 as though he were writing in 1950—as though he were unconscious of anything, any experiment in language or form, that had happened in between.

The subordination of feeling or drama to a formal arrangement is as marked in Douglas Crase's *The Revisionist*. I don't mind a poet's using a mannered style—Yeats, for instance, could be very grand—but I object to verbosity, and Crase is verbose. And he uses abstract language:

For a person, it gets to be a matter of concern
Being the transport of too many arguments not your own
And under a season patiently endured . . .

so that his argument is obscure—and he is always arguing. But in fact, what this writing produces is not a line of argument but a sound. It is what philosophy sounds like. As with the later poems of Wallace Stevens, to understand what Crase is saying you would have to study the poem—you cannot grasp it as a whole, sound and meaning both, while his ponderous sentences are unrolling. That is to say, there is the disassociation of sensibility, split between sound and meaning, Eliot pointed to fifty years ago. Some poets and critics actually seem to prefer it—this is why Stevens has been having a vogue. They prefer ratiocination to the kind of involvement that lyrical and dramatic poetry demands.

The following passage by Crase will show what I mean when I say that he is producing the *sound* of philosophy—lulling, no doubt, to those who like it.

> So many versions at any time are all exemplary
> (In fog, suspended drops of rain; in a blizzard,
> Each driven crystal the authentic apotheosis of the snow)
> It is impossible to choose, to even want to choose
> From millions of improbably accurate identities,
> Things as they are. Selection magnifies, but concurrently
> It excludes and how can that be satisfactory
> When present estates, so-called, include all recollections
> Of what they were as well as the motives for remembering
> them?
>
> ("The Lake Effect")

Throughout his book Crase refers to topography, geology, and the weather in order to raise questions about the nature of perception. But we don't arrive at any insights, for ideas in poems have no effect unless they are realized in images or embodied in an action we can see and feel.

Jared Carter is at the opposite extreme from Crase and McClatchy, taking his place with the poets who create images and may even create characters and a story. The poems in *Work, for the Night Is Coming* are about small-town lives. He owes something to Rousseau and Wordsworth, finding virtue in rural scenes and people who are almost inarticulate. It is an American tradition to find poetry in such scenes—one group of poems titled "Tintypes," a series of monologues delivered by the dead, is strongly reminiscent of *Spoon River*. Sam Bass, "train robber and outlaw," describes the manner of his dying:

> It took three days for me to bleed to death.
> People crowded around the shack
> Where they had me, but I never talked.

He concludes,

> If a man knows anything
> He ought to die with it in him.

This poetry is plain-spoken and as hard as ten-penny nails.

Carter will have to guard against another American tradition that ties in with sympathy for the inarticulate—the tendency to say nothing at all. In order to offset this he develops a significant, emotive ending, as in the lines quoted above, moving the poem outward. This could lead to moralizing, however. His best writing is in lines that present experience just as it is:

> There is the bar where she went each night to sit
> There is the sparkling SCHLITZ sign over the mirror
> There is the jukebox that only works if you kick it.
>
> ("Walking the Ties")

This is how poetry is found in America, not in some green pastoral scene. But it takes courage to hang in there. No wonder some poets would like to escape in artificial language, a structure and style as far removed from speech as possible. As Baudelaire said, "Anywhere . . . out of the world."

News from the North, Memories of the Tropics

The West Indian culture into which Derek Walcott was born was Janus-faced: one face that of an Englishman, the other that of a native of St. Lucia. At present Walcott is living in the United States. The poetry in which he writes about the Caribbean is lyrical and full of bright images, lines shimmering like the sea. Even an approaching hurricane may yield pleasures of sight and sound.

> Once branching light startles the hair of the coconuts,
> and on the villas' asphalt roofs, rain
> resonates like pebbles in a pan . . .

Transported to Manhattan, he writes: "I lead a tight life / and a cold one, my soles stiffen with ice. . . ." The question is how to retain the delight in physical existence of his Caribbean heritage and at the same time come to grips with the North . . . industrial, winter-bitten, sinister. "The weevil," he writes, "will make a sahara of Kansas, / the ant shall eat Russia." For the North, it appears, lacks charity.

The opening poem, "Old New England," shows one of the ways in which he has tried to manage the transition from the

---

This review of *The Fortunate Traveller* by Derek Walcott appeared in the *Washington Post Book World*, February 21, 1982.

warm South to the cold North. He writes in the manner of Robert Lowell:

> Black clippers, tarred with whales' blood, fold their sails
> entering New Bedford, New London, New Haven.
> A white church spire whistles into space . . .

This is the very language and imagery of Lowell's "The Quaker Graveyard in Nantucket." I find it astonishing that a poet of Walcott's talent should write in frank imitation of another man's style. What can he hope to accomplish by these poems except to have it said that they sound like Lowell's?

No, there is an American language, just as there is a West Indian, and Walcott will have to find it. He overcame a stuffy British colonial background to develop his own lyrical style. It will require as much work again to write poems about the United States in an authentic voice. One of the perils of being a traveler is that you may be adopted by someone on the first day out whom you can't get rid of for the rest of the trip. Walcott had better shake off Lowell's influence and get on with writing in a style of his own.

These imitations aside, *The Fortunate Traveller* contains several poems that are brilliantly written. As someone once remarked to me, Walcott is a spellbinder. Of how many poets can it be said that their poems are compelling—not a mere stringing together of images and ideas but language that delights in itself, rhythms that seem spontaneous, scenes that are vividly there?

As the title indicates, these poems are set in different places. Walcott seems to feel that he needs a "public" voice in order to speak with authority about the many things, not necessarily connected, he has seen and heard in his travels. He says of himself, "I, whose ancestors were slave and Roman, / have seen both sides of the imperial foam." This is a little too orotund. A more persuasive voice is heard in poems such as "Easter" and "Store Bay" that appear to be about personal matters. And it is imagining with sympathy, not a wish to speak publicly, that enables him to reconstruct the childhood of Jean Rhys, another brilliant West Indian:

> A maiden aunt canoes through lilies of clouds
> in a Carib hammock, to a hymn's metronome . . .

Sensuality mixed with religion . . . the history of a culture in two lines. The poet who can write like this is a master.

Dramas and Confessions

For a generation, American poetry has been stuck in the first person like a truck spinning its wheels. A few poets, however, have gone beyond the confessional and, in writing about themselves, have made up stories. The "I" in the poem is treated as a character, and life is given a more dramatic, satisfying shape. That is the way Robert Lowell wrote *Life Studies,* and in *Tar* C. K. Williams appears to be transforming the worlds of adolescence and early manhood in the same fashion.

He uses a long line with eight stresses—at least by my count—that carries the action steadily forward, allows for the inclusion of details and creates a music apart from what the writing is about. You are conscious of the pace and sound of verse, though the material is the kind you expect to find in a novel:

A low, gray frame building, it was gloomy and rundown, but
  charmingly old-fashioned:
ancient wooden floors, open shelves, the smell of unwrapped
  candy, cigarettes and bandaid glue.

Such is the accuracy of description that I recognize the bus station in Pennsylvania Mr. Williams has in mind. I don't mean the type but the particular specimen.

Mr. Williams is a realist. Reading "Combat," which describes the narrator's frustrating and unforgettable affair with a young woman who is a German refugee—an affair encouraged by her mother—we feel this is how it must have been because it is grotesque. The grotesque is the sign of truth in our time.

His realism spares us nothing. If you want to know what a cripple looks like with his pants down, Mr. Williams will tell you. But if you want the breath of spring on parted lips, you're out of luck. The muse of poetry Whitman saw arriving in the United States has been with us for some time, as Whitman said, "install'd amid the kitchenware," but I am inclined to think the Graces haven't arrived and, given our Puritan hatred of beauty, never may.

Several of Mr. Williams's poems make a point about suffering and doubt and the moments of expanded consciousness that suffering and doubt occasionally produce. One of his memorable successes is the title poem, "Tar"—perhaps because the material is so resistant to poetry and yet he manages to make poetry out of it. As Doctor Johnson said, nothing good is achieved without difficulty.

> The first morning of Three Mile Island: those first disquiet-
> ing, uncertain, mystifying hours.
> All morning a crew of workmen have been tearing the old
> decrepit roof off our building.

How can removing an old roof and the near catastrophe of Three Mile Island be connected? The poem manages to connect them:

> I remember a woman on the front page glaring across the
> misty Susquehanna at those looming stacks.
> But, more vividly, the men, silvered with glitter from the
> shingles, clinging like starlings beneath the eaves.

Even the leftover carats of tar in the gutter, so black they
　　seemed to suck the light out of the air.
By nightfall kids had come across them: every sidewalk on
　　the block was scribbled with obscenities and hearts.

We get the message. This is Mr. Williams's fable for the
nuclear age, his statement of faith in perdurable, blundering
humanity. It is also a statement of faith in the art he practices—poetry "scribbled with obscenities and hearts" and as
hard as lumps of tar. A number of poets are putting characters and incidents in their poems and reclaiming territory that
had been abandoned to the novel. C. K. Williams is in the
front rank of the movement.

It used to be said that the aim of poetry is to give pleasure or
instruction, but there is a kind of writing that expresses mis-
ery. Some years ago, there was a school of poets for whom
insanity and suicide were favorite subjects. They were called
"extremist" and "confessional." This is the genre to which
Frank Bidart has contributed with *The Sacrifice*.

The book opens with a dramatic monologue in verse, sup-
posedly spoken by the dancer Vaslav Nijinsky, who had gone
insane. Mr. Bidart intersperses his verse with prose explana-
tions and one of these informs us that in 1919 Nijinsky invited
guests to a recital: "When the audience was seated, he picked
up a chair, sat down on it, and stared at them. Half an hour
passed. Then he took a few rolls of black and white velvet and
made a big cross the length of the room. He stood at the head
of it, his arms opened wide. He said: 'Now, I will dance you
the War, which you did not prevent and for which you are
responsible.' His dance reflected battle, horror, catastrophe,
apocalypse."

A monologue leads up to this incident, with Nijinsky remi-
niscing, wondering whether he is insane or evil and
concluding:

I must join MY GUILT

to the WORLD'S GUILT.

Mr. Bidart must find Nijinsky's mind fascinating, for he gives it to us straight. But if this was Nijinsky, when it came to expressing himself in words he had two left feet. There is no visual imagination in the writing and no music. Here is Nijinsky speaking—he refers to himself in the third person—at once hysterical and banal:

> he LEARNED SOMETHING.
>
> He learned that
>
> *All life exists*
>
> *at the expense of other life* . . .

"Confessional," again in the form of a monologue, describes a tangled family relationship—son, mother, father, and stepfather. The mother has had spells of insanity. The son is trying to communicate, as they say on television:

> but no,—
> she *couldn't* forgive me . . .
>
> WHY COULDN'T SHE FORGIVE ME?

There is analyzing of motive and character in terms you might hear at a cocktail party:

> The emotions, the "*issues*" in her life
> didn't come out somewhere, reached no culmination,
> climax, catharsis,—
>
> she *JUST DIED.*

In the title poem, "The Sacrifice," Mr. Bidart's thoughts about Judas and Jesus are murkily attached to the story of a

> Miss Mary Kenwood; who, without
> help, placed her head in a plastic bag.
>
> then locked herself
> in a refrigerator.

The concluding poem, "Genesis 1-2:4," retells the creation of the world:

God said,
> LET THE WATERS BELOW THE FIRMAMENT
> RECEDE, REVEALING THE GROUND.

The waters opened, and receded.
What lay beneath the waters was the GROUND.

But as Mr. Bidart is always strident, his "Genesis" falls flat. He lacks the essential quality for a poet who wishes to move the reader to tears or fill him with awe—a sense of humor.

The Aeneid

The Roman poet Publius Vergilius Maro, whom we call Virgil, modeled his epic poem about the origins of Rome on Homer's *Iliad* and *Odyssey*. But the Greeks in Homer were a disparate and quarrelsome lot—the ancestors of the Romans would be bound together by a sense of national destiny.

The Aeneid describes the fall of Troy and tells how a band of survivors wandered in the eastern Mediterranean, settled in Italy and overcame their enemies in battle.

The narrative is filled with scene and incident, and Virgil writes like a mason fitting one perfect stone to another. But the poem also has been read for its didactic passages and moral uplift. Like the hero of HMS *Pinafore,* the hero of Virgil's poem rejects "all temptations / To belong to other nations." He cleaves to duty and his persistence is finally rewarded.

Aeneas is tempted by Dido, queen of Carthage, to stay in Africa and forget his purpose. They have a passionate affair. Ordered by the gods to leave at once, Aeneas makes his apologies to the queen.

> I never shall deny all you can say,
> Your majesty, of what you meant to me.

But the woman is enraged; she calls him perfidious. In order to avoid further confrontations, Aeneas leaves the

This review of *The Aeneid,* translated by Robert Fitzgerald, appeared in *USA Today,* December 19, 1983.

country by stealth. Dido then climbs to the top of a pyre and kills herself with a sword.

There are other temptations. The ghost of Aeneas's father warns him that Romans must not devote themselves to art, rhetoric, or astronomy.

> Others will cast more tenderly in bronze
> Their breathing figures, I can well believe,
> And bring more lifelike portraits out of marble;
> Argue more eloquently, use the pointer
> To trace the paths of heaven accurately . . .

Romans have something more important to do than dabble in the liberal arts. "Your arts," says Anchises, "are to be these":

> To pacify, to impose the rule of law,
> To spare the conquered, battle down the proud.

This has been the creed held by conquerors and empire-builders throughout history.—"Our will is law."

The descriptions in Fitzgerald's translations are lively and clear. The ship race is exciting and he gives some variety to the battle scenes. It's here one feels that Virgil is imitating Homer without Homer's zest for hand-to-hand combat. But Fitzgerald makes the fighting real.

> Pallas put a javelin
> Through him where the spine divides the ribs,
> Then pulled it from the cage of bone it clung to.

This new version of *The Aeneid* is not without faults. The opening words, *"Arma virumque cano"* (literally, "Arms and the man I sing"), Fitzgerald translates, "I sing of warfare and a man at war." But it is not Aeneas solely in his capacity as warrior that Virgil is evoking—Aeneas also is the man chosen by destiny and, in a more personal sense, the one who has gone through all this. Whitman's line gives the feel of it: "I am the man, I suffer'd, I was there."

But it is in translating Virgil's aphorisms, those trenchant lines that have come down through the ages, that Fitzgerald seems to lack inspiration. *"Possunt, quia posse videntur"* he translates, "Who felt that they could do it, and so could," a phrase no one would want to remember. Rolfe Humphries, in his version of *The Aeneid*, translated the line as it had been translated for generations: "They can because they think they can."

Fitzgerald is a considerable poet in his own right. His poems evoke Virgilian shadows, constellations shining above the sea, "the tears of things." He is therefore able to bring out the elegiac side of Virgil. For Virgil is the poet of the underworld as well as the brilliant surface.

Aeneas himself seems curiously divided. He is not a primitive hero—not at all Homeric—he is more like a man of our time, conscientious and perplexed. Fitzgerald has a good phrase for this: Aeneas is "the dedicated man."

Fitzgerald's ear for the living word makes his translation of *The Aeneid* a pleasure to read and Aeneas a more attractive hero than "pious Aeneas," the prig we learned about in school.

Friends and Opinions and Influences

The imagination, Donald Davie says, is concerned with "one particular person, in one place, at one time, in one sort of weather." Therefore he is re-creating the individuals, some of them obscure, and the places, some well off the beaten path, that contributed to his growth as a writer. He is speaking of "companions," individuals who have meant something to him personally, rather than those he has met in his career as poet, teacher, and critic. Like the Russian novelists he admires, he aims to render things as they were. He is not drawing morals, for, he says, he does not have "the heart for it," but is making a truthful record so that the people, places, and times he is describing may invite "different reflections from those of the narrator." In this I think he has succeeded, for as I read about his adventures and considered his reflections, my reflections were frequently very different from his.

Donald Davie grew up in Barnsley, a town in Yorkshire, and he has remained, he tells us, temperamentally of the North of England, "the region of the stripped and the straitened, the necessitous." His father was a shopkeeper and a deacon in the Baptist church; he had a flair for comic mime and impersonation. His mother was born in a colliery cottage; she was devoted to poetry, and so young Donald Davie grew up "literary." Clever at taking examinations, he obtained a scholarship to Cambridge. After a spell in the Navy during World War II, he returned to Cambridge to take a degree. There he came under the influence of the fiercely moralizing F. R. Leavis. Men of his generation, Mr. Davie tells us, did not find release when they were discharged from military service but went into harness in order to make a career.

Mr. Davie's frankness about this and other matters invites a certain sort of reader to feel superior. He says that he has been a "coward before life," a prig and a prude. To write so doubtfully about oneself is to put a weapon in the hands of envy and malice. Most writers only admit to failings—promiscuous sexual activity, for example—that most people do not regard as failings. In reading Mr. Davie's admissions, I had, as it were, to protect him from himself, from his zeal for explaining his limitations. He is not a prig now, if he ever was. He is not a "coward before life." He is a writer, and a writer can't immerse himself in human relationships but must stand a little way off. About prudishness, however, I think he may be right. He tells us that sex is "in the last analysis comical" and that Joyce's *Ulysses,* though great, is a "smutty and sniggering book." Apparently he missed the comic passages.

When he was growing up in Barnsley, he was taught to fear "rough boys." But in the Navy he had to deal with them and found that he enjoyed their company. One was lazy and salacious; another pilfered articles from packing cases; and Mr. Davie uncovered in himself a streak of sympathy: "I liked the imprudent ones far more than the reliable and responsible." He has a recurring suspicion, not uncommon among writers, that the nonliterary, even philistine, individual has a more immediate relationship with truth than the educated. As Flaubert said of a bourgeois family, "They are in the right." This may be why, in the face of political aggression from left or right, intellectuals have been known to grovel while street cleaners stood fast.

This last is my reflection, not Mr. Davie's. On this subject—the pros and cons of having an imagination—he is an expert. Is it possible, he muses, that the stability of the English—

demonstrated by their resistance to the Nazis—came of their inability to imagine defeat? Other peoples with a more vivid imagination (the Poles and Irish, for example) have paid a terrible price for having it. But, he asks, is survival the test of the validity of attitudes and ideas? Here, on the verge of chaos or perhaps of a revelation, Mr. Davie ceases to pursue his train of thought.

This is where I find him dissatisfying. Sometimes I get the feeling from Mr. Davie's reflections that I have had in conversations with English men and women, that they retire behind a wall of "good taste." You think you are having a discussion and find you are at a club. "Who outside England," says Mr. Davie, "thinks any longer that the making of a point is what a poem can or should be concerned with?" I could tell him, but he does not stay for an answer. Yeats's rhyming of "Lissadell" and "gazelle," he remarks, is "the most triumphantly audacious rhyme in modern English." There is no British writer he adores more than Kingsley Amis. And I have already mentioned his opinion of *Ulysses*.

Speaking of critics who emasculate poetry by treating it as though it were prose, Mr. Davie says, "I could name names, and they would be distinguished ones." Why doesn't he name them?

The trouble with this kind of reticence is that judgements seem to be made on the basis of personal taste rather than thought. Yet Mr. Davie's range of sympathy is impressive. He has written about Ezra Pound at one extreme and Thomas Hardy at the other. American writers, on the other hand, seem to know only one thing, and few in universities can write a book that anyone wants to read. Mr. Davie's recollections are very readable; in fact, one is likely to go through them too fast, looking for nuggets. The chapters about Russia during the war, when he was stationed at Polyarno and Archangel on the Arctic Circle, have the realism and a sense of spiritual space corresponding to the immensity of the land that one finds in Russian writing. The people are equally memorable—best of all, a statuesque Russian woman with a can of sugared beer in one hand and a raw fish in the other. Mr.

Davie also captures the atmosphere of Trinity College, Dublin, and landscapes in California and Italy.

Some of his companions are legendary—that is, in literary circles—and not much is known about them. Here are the people to go with the names: the neglected Irish poet Austin Clarke, ironic and self-defeating; the American poet and critic Yvor Winters, whose "small travelling bag swung from his hand with an unhappy excess of assumed carelessness" and who "glared at me mistrustfully through strong lenses." I thoroughly enjoyed his description of Winters telling him about the greatness of Robert Bridges, the English poet, and how Yeats was overrated. Winters would have fitted in Gogol's novel of provincial clowns and grotesques.

Mr. Davie laments the disappearance of the "literary civilisation" he grew up in; the idea of a civilization of readers is now "discredited and mocked almost universally." Writers who spend much time in universities are likely to grow despondent over the future of literature, for there it is treated as a finished thing. The answer is to know the kind of people outside universities whose feelings and ideas are raw—the stuff that poetry is made of. Thanks to his temperament, Mr. Davie has always been drawn from literature back to life where she stands, a can of beer in one hand, a fish in the other. In spite of his dim view of the future of literacy, he enjoys the act of writing, and cheerfulness keeps breaking in.

Conrad in the Nineteenth Century

Fiction, Conrad said, appeals to temperament, and his critics have been temperamental. A brilliantly intuitive reading of the text will be followed by a reading, no less intuitive, that strikes one as wide of the mark. This may be why V. S. Naipaul has said, "Perhaps it doesn't matter what we say about Conrad; it is enough that he is discussed." One is tempted to agree—does not Conrad's view of the art of fiction reject interpretation? His work, he said, was not "an endless analysis of affected sentiments"—the kind of writing that lends itself to interpretation. It consisted of action, "nothing but action—action observed, felt, and interpreted with an absolute truth to my sensations (which are the basis of art in literature)."

If this is true of Conrad's fiction, and I believe it is, then the most helpful criticism will be that which gives us the information we need in order to form our own ideas, rather than the kind that displays the originality of the critic. Ian Watt has given us that book. He is able to give us a "new" reading of a passage by Conrad, but that is not his aim—his aim, rather, is to show what may legitimately be derived from the words on the page, and from our knowledge of history. If he strikes us as original, and from time to time he strikes us as very original indeed, this is a byproduct of his search for the truth. This is more than a book of criticism of Conrad's novels and stories—it is a work from which young men and women who wish to be critics could learn their trade.

This review of *Conrad in the Nineteenth Century* by Ian Watt appeared in *Novel, A Forum on Fiction* 15, no. 3 (Spring 1982).

The writer appeals to temperament, the critic appeals to history. Watt opens with an account of Conrad's childhood in Poland. His family were of the Polish nobility, the *szlachta*. In later years "Conrad must have discovered an unexpected congruence between his life as a ship's officer and some of his inherited expectations as a member of the *szlachta*. His pay and his life ashore might be dismal and humiliating, but on board the officers' mess and the attentions of the steward provided a framework of privileged status for his daily life." Observations such as these, made in a few sentences, tell us more about Conrad's life and its relation to his work than whole chapters of other men's books.

Watt himself raises the question of the right aim and method of literary criticism, drawing firm boundaries between criticism and the expression of one's personal ideas or fantasies. "The modern critical tendency to decompose literary works into a series of more or less cryptic references to a system of non-literal unifying meanings is in large part a misguided response to a very real problem in the interpretation of much modern literature." He goes on to explain: "The expressive idiom of modern writing in general is characterised by an insistent separateness between the particular items of experience presented and the reader's need to generate larger connecting meanings out of them." Into this gap, then, rushes the literary critic, whose task is to explain to the public "in discursive expository prose a literature whose expressive idiom was intended to be inaccessible to exposition in any conceptual terms." Conrad's idea of writing, in other words, that would be "nothing but action."

Many critics are not content to throw a bridge over the gap—they fill it with rubble. "The modern critic," Watt says, "finds it easy to succumb to the temptation of discovering hidden allegorical configurations, thereby laying himself open to the charge of excessive abstraction or extravagant symbol-hunting." I would add that this is why many writers do not read literary criticism of a kind that is written these days—it strikes them as a distortion of the whole aim of writing. It is an obstacle between the reader and the text. There are some highly publicized critics who claim that their own interpretations or misreadings of the text are all that matters. This is a hopeful sign—in literature and literary criticism those whom the gods wish to destroy they first make fashionable. But *Conrad in the Nineteenth Century* may be a sign that things are beginning to change, returning literary criticism to the author and the reader.

Watt's sense of history enables him, as I have said, to read texts in a new way. For example, he knows about solidarity as a historical movement, and this enables him to give us a new reading of Conrad's preface to *The Nigger of the Narcissus*. The passage critics usually fasten upon is Conrad's ringing declaration of his intention "by the power of the written word to make you hear, to make you feel . . . before all, to make you *see*." This is fine, and most readers of Conrad, having read this, may think that they have understood the preface. Watt gives the famous passage its due but also directs the reader's attention to another place that is never mentioned. What, after all, is the purpose of making you hear, feel, and see? What is the use of fiction? Surely this is an important question, one that all writers have asked themselves, and many readers. Ford Madox Ford said that the aim of writing fiction was to create an illusion of life, but why he did not say. Watt directs the reader to the passage in which Conrad hopes that his writing will "awaken in the hearts of the beholders that feeling of unavoidable solidarity; of the solidarity in mysterious origin, in toil, in joy, in hope, in uncertain fate, which binds men to each other and all mankind to the visible world."

This reading of the preface enables us to read Conrad with a lesser emphasis on his despair and a greater emphasis on his trust in mankind. The margin will always be narrow—in every story by Conrad there is a Decoud who may very well jump into the sea—but Conrad is not so insistently a writer of "nerves" as he has been painted. Baudelaire spoke of "les sterilités des écrivains nerveux," and critics who pride themselves on being modern and nervous have seized upon Conrad's nervousness and his sterilities. But as Watt has remarked elsewhere, how could the hypochondriac they describe have written all the novels and stories? If, on the other hand, we think of "solidarity," and read Conrad in the light of his expressed purpose, we begin to see that his writing is sustained by more than nervous energy. One might, *pace* E. M. Forster, say that Conrad has a consistent point of view, almost a "philosophy."

It is more than this—it gives him a method, a way of structuring the inchoate mass of experience and turning it into fiction. And it gives us a way of seeing the structure of his fiction. Conrad's aim is to create some scene, gesture, moment of action so intensely that he will bind the reader to him, and his readers to one another. We may not know for certain what Kurtz did, and every time we try to understand the chronology of *Nostromo* we may come up with different figures, but these are only matters of fact—they are "life," which is confusing. Life does not "bind men to each other and all mankind to the visible world." Only imagination can do that. Moments of experience observed by the author and re-created so that they may be shared by his readers, create a feeling of solidarity. These moments of binding are the real action.

The quality of the writing in *Conrad in the Nineteenth Century* cannot be praised too highly. Apart from an extended passage on "decoding"—what in movies would be called a "double take"—I find very little of the special language of literary criticism. In reading Ian Watt one has the impression, as with criticism of only the highest caliber, that other and perhaps more striking ways of saying a thing have been sacrificed in order to write accurate and truthful sentences.

The opening sections on the historical background, Conrad's early life, the literary models he had before him, culminate with the question: "Alienation, of course; but how do we get out of it?" Watt's originality will lie in his considering the second half of the question—others have been content with alienation. In the epilogue he picks up the question again, to explain Conrad's importance at the present time: ". . . in a solitude that was not merely exile Conrad had extracted from his inheritance of loss and alienation a deep understanding of the need for moral resistance and affirmation, a need whose subsequent topicality neither he nor his contemporaries could possibly have imagined."

The novels and stories are discussed in the order of their appearance, and social or literary matters are explained when they have a bearing on the work in hand. Solidarity, political and ideological, is explained in relation to *The Nigger of the Narcissus*. Discussions of colonialism and of literary impressionism and symbolism precede the discussion of *Heart of Darkness*.

Much of the information we shall need in order to understand Conrad's later writing has already been provided in this first volume. Therefore the task remaining is not as formidable as it may seem to the author. The second volume will deal with *Nostromo, The Secret Agent,* "The Secret Sharer," *Under Western Eyes, The Shadow Line,* and the works of Conrad's so-called decline. Readers of *Conrad in the Nineteenth Century* are looking forward to what Ian Watt has to tell them of Conrad in the twentieth.

Disorder and Escape in the
Fiction of V. S. Naipaul

To be born on an island like Isabella . . . was to be born to disorder.
                                                            The Mimic Men

The greater part of the fiction of V. S. Naipaul is set in the newly independent states of Africa and the Caribbean, and the view is pessimistic: the natives have taken the government into their own hands but are unable to establish order. As Robert Boyers has observed, "Naipaul is our primary novelist of disorder and breakdown."[1]

But though the novels offer controversial views of life in the new states this is not why they are compelling. In art it is the mind of the artist that makes the difference, his own interest in the work he is creating. Boyers remarks that Naipaul "seems more interested in a spiritual or psychological state than in the machinery of action," and I would add that the spiritual or psychological state he is most interested in is his own.

As a child Vidyadha Naipaul grew up in a big house in Chaguanas, a community of East Indians whose forebears had immigrated to Trinidad as indentured laborers. They perpetuated Indian rituals and marriage customs, and had little contact with the world outside—with the Negroes, for example.[2] But Vidyadha's father, Seepersad Naipaul, was different—he was a writer of newspaper articles. And he was

---

This essay first appeared in the *Hudson Review* 37, no. 4 (Winter 1984–85).

exceedingly troubled—he did not get along with his wife's family. His son tells us that these in-laws were a "totalitarian organization. Decisions—about politics, about religious matters, and, most important, about other families—were taken to a closed circle at the top—my grandmother and her two eldest sons-in-law."[3]

The recurring theme of Naipaul's fiction, the need to escape from a "totalitarian" environment, was the obsession of his father, and of course Naipaul has shown it to be so in *A House for Mr. Biswas*. For house read a separate life.

Seepersad Naipaul challenged Hindu beliefs and superstitions. He informed his readers that native farmers were practicing rites of Kali in order to cure their diseased cattle. Thereupon he received an anonymous letter in Hindi warning him that he would develop poisoning, "die on Sunday and be buried on Monday," unless he offered the sacrifice of a goat to Kali. He made the sacrifice. This, his son observes, was a great humiliation. "It had occurred just when my father was winning through to a kind of independence."

When Vidyadha was six his father moved his family into Port of Spain. This was "in the nature of a migration from the Hindu and Indian countryside to the white-Negro-mulatto town." The child was delighted with the sights and sounds and characters—men like Bogart, who had shaken off Hindu family conventions and taken a new name from the movies.

But Seepersad Naipaul's bid for independence was aborted. His mother-in-law bought a cocoa estate in the hills to the northwest of Port of Spain, and "it was decided—by the people in the family who decided on such matters—that the whole family . . . should move there." So the freedoms of the town were suspended and made way again for family quarrels.

After two years of this Seepersad Naipaul moved his family back to Port of Spain where he managed to have a job with the government. But they were living crowded into rooms and the street was changing. There was an American military base at the end of the street—one of the houses or yards had become a brothel. "Disorder within," says the novelist, "disorder without. Only my school life was ordered; anything that had happened there I could date at once. But my family life—my life at home or my life in the house, in the street—was jumbled, without sequence."

There must have been much in the street to appall him. He had been brought up by people who were scrupulously clean and who disapproved strongly of sexual relations with non-Hindus. The characters in Naipaul's fiction echo these attitudes. In *The Mimic Men* Singh tells how as a boy he used a girl's toothbrush by mistake—"I felt," he says, "dreadfully unclean." In *An Area of Darkness* Naipaul remembers that once in a science class he would not suck on a length of tube that had been touched by other mouths, and another Indian boy in the class remarked approvingly, "Real brahmin." As for habits that are obviously unsanitary, such as defecating in the streets, Naipaul's revulsion is memorable. Everything else he has to say about life in India pales in comparison with the strength of his feelings on this subject.

One can imagine the mingled fear and fascination of the young Hindu when confronted with the sexual disorder of Port of Spain, the "brothel ground" at the end of the street.

"Only my school life was ordered." The school was Queen's Royal College, which appears in *The Mimic Men* as Isabella Imperial. The headmaster was an Englishman; the curriculum would have been that of a public school in England. Discipline would have been firm, with "lines" for lesser derelictions and caning for more serious offenses.

A colonial education such as this offered a good deal of security. In Naipaul's *Guerillas* the writer Roche says that he is not usually afraid, and attributes this to his having been educated at a British school. "It's the way I am. It probably has to do with the school I went to. I suppose if you accept authority and believe in the rules, you aren't afraid of any particular individual."

Queen's Royal College offered Naipaul a refuge from the disorder at home and in the streets. And his education taught him the value of order. If he was like other young men and women who were educated in the colonies, he came to think that the Mother Country was the pattern of a good society. And it would follow that other places were inferior. The more he studied English history and literature, the more he would feel that the culture of the Caribbean—if it could be called a culture at all—was inferior. Such was the inevitable result of an education in a British colony. England was the real world to which colonials might aspire, but they could never hope to be included. The history of the West Indies was not real history, the English they spoke was not as correct as that spoken in England. The grass was greener in Sussex and the birds sang more sweetly.

Naipaul traveled to England on a government scholarship and studied at Oxford. The descriptions of the immigrant's life in *The Mimic Men* shows how disillusioning that life could be. Nothing would have prepared the West Indian for the English climate or the dreariness of living in a boarding house. Confronted with greasy wallpaper and a gas meter into which you had to feed shillings to keep warm, he would have had long thoughts.

Outside you were overwhelmed by the monuments and public buildings that seemed to be saying that you had no part in the centuries. It takes more than a public school education to make you English—you have to have been born in England.

Some of the immigrants, in order to keep their self-respect, withdrew from the life around them. The narrator of *A Bend in the River* observes: "Indar had said about people like me that when we came to a great city we closed our eyes; we were concerned only to show that we were not amazed."

At this point Naipaul became a writer. Going to Queen's Royal College was his first escape from disorder—writing was his second. Ever since he was a child he had wanted to be a writer like his father, who wrote articles for the *Trinidad Guardian* about "village feuds, family vendettas, murders, bitter election battles." He wrote about strange characters such as a Negro hermit who had once been rich and pleasure-seeking but now lived alone with a dog in a hut in the swamplands. "I read the stories as stories," Naipaul remarks—a hint, perhaps, to those who would read his own fiction as something else.[4]

Naipaul's first novels, *The Mystic Masseur* and *The Suffrage of Elvira,* are about people and events such as his father described. The Mystic Masseur was not farfetched: there was a Camār from Janglī Tolā—that is, an East Indian of lower caste—who "set himself up as a Brahman pundit." In writing about the Mystic Masseur, also, Naipaul was reenacting his own escape by way of an education. "This reading," says one of the characters in *The Mystic Masseur,* "is a great great thing."

Naipaul's *Mr. Stone and the Knights Companion,* which might have been written by J. B. Priestley—it seems like an exercise in writing a perfectly English novel in order to prove that he could do it—has one lively passage in which Mr. Stone discovers the joy of writing. This it is that gives meaning to his existence—he is never so happy again as when composing the plan for the Knights Companion. "He wrote, he corrected, he re-wrote; and fatigue never came to him." Afterwards "He felt exhausted, sad and empty."

This was how it felt to escape from life into writing. And the following sentences about Mr. Stone's writing strike me as Naipaul's own thoughts about the art he practices: "The only pure moments, the only true moments were those he had spent in the study, writing out of a feeling whose depths he realized only as he wrote." Then Naipaul observes: "What he had written was a faint and artificial rendering of that emotion, and the scheme as the Unit had practiced it was but a shadow of that shadow. All passion had disappeared. . . . All action, all creation was a betrayal of feeling and truth.

But unlike other writers without a cause, Naipaul does not make a religion of his art. Eugene Goodheart surmises that Naipaul would scorn "the Flaubertian dream of a perfect work of art, which is all form and no content."[5] I would put it another way: while Naipaul appears to find the act of writing completely satisfying, he is not attached to the results.

Naipaul has told how he hit on a subject. He had left Oxford and was working for the BBC Caribbean service in London, presenting a weekly literary program for the Caribbean. One day when he was sitting in the dimly lighted "freelances' room" his thoughts reverted to Port of Spain and he typed the sentence: "Every morning when he got up Hat would sit on the banister of his back verandah and shout across, 'What happening there, Bogart?' " The story thus begun led to other stories. *Miguel Street* was written quickly.[6] He was putting a part of his life behind him, an area of darkness.

This is what gives Naipaul's fiction its compelling power. He is always putting darkness behind him. As he has made his escape from disorder, first through his education, then through writing, in his novels and stories people struggle to escape. Sometimes they do escape and sometimes they don't. In the novel titled *In a Free State* the Africans have taken over from the white people. Bobby and Linda, who are white, are driving toward the safety of the European compound. "Somewhere up there," says Linda, "they've taken off their nice new clothes and they're dancing naked and holding hands and eating dung." Bobby and Linda meet up with a group of native soldiers who humiliate and beat the white man, but they manage to reach the compound. In *Guerillas* the woman Jane becomes involved sexually with the leader of the guerillas—that is, they call themselves guerillas, but the writer Roche calls them a gang. Jane is leaving the island, but she makes a detour to say goodbye to her lover and is murdered. Her annihilation is total—her body will never be found.

The narrator of *A Bend in the River* manages to escape from the new state, but many do not. As the steamer travels into the sunset he sees dugouts full of people who are desperately trying to tie up to the steamer. "They were in flight from the riverbanks. They jammed and jostled against the sides of the steamer and the barge, and many were swamped. Water hyacinths pushed up in the narrow space between the steamer and the barge. We went on. Darkness fell."

The plot I have described is that of a nightmare. As Nazruddin says in *A Bend in the River*, "You can always get into those places. What is hard is to get out." He makes the further observation: "That is a private fight. Everybody has to find his own way." Naipaul has found his own way—the characters in his fiction sometimes do not. In any case, we share their anxiety, the pressure to escape. We hurry to the end of a novel by Naipaul as we hurry to the end of a nightmare. Anything, even confrontation with the worst, is better than being in suspense.

We are between two worlds, the old order that has ended, the new order that has not begun. Naipaul is the novelist of the state in between—a state that is psychological as well as political. I have tried to describe the psychology because I think it more likely to last.

The characters in Naipaul's fiction may be planning for a future state, but the writer is not to be identified with his characters. He resists absorption by any place or nation. In *An Area of Darkness* Naipaul speaks of an Indian "philosophy of despair, leading to passivity, detachment, acceptance. It is only now," he remarks, "as the impatience of the observer is dissipated in the processes of writing and self-inquiry, that I see how much this philosophy had also been mine. It had enabled me through the stresses of a long residence in England, to withdraw completely from nationality and loyalties except to persons; it had made me content to be myself alone, my work, my name (the last two so different from the first); it had convinced me that every man was an island, and taught me to shield all that I knew to be good and pure within myself from the corruption of causes."

The protagonist in a novel by Naipaul is escaping but does not hope to arrive—he knows there is no great, good place. I am reminded of the writing of another novelist, Joseph Conrad. Conrad grew up in Poland under Russian occupation; his father was enlisted in the hopeless cause of revolution. G. Jean-Aubry says of Conrad in his early years, "Unconsciously he was being trained in a secret and inflexible fidelity to ideals disassociated from hope."[7] The same might be said of Naipaul. In his writing there is a conflict between intellectual curiosity, a first-rate reporter's interest in the way people live, and a tremendous passivity, a conviction of the futility of intelligence . . . its weakness when confronted with brute force.

Like Conrad, Naipaul has chosen to live in England where people leave you alone and you need have no loyalty except to persons. In this neutral environment he is able to write novels that reenact his escape from disorder and his father's struggle to escape. The novels tell us how corrupt and violent life can be, and that it is necessary to fly from others in order to preserve all that is "good and pure" within oneself.

Flowers and weeds cling to the boat, and a thousand hands reach out to hold it back.

NOTES

1. Robert Boyers, "V. S. Naipaul," *American Scholar* (Summer 1981): 118, 366.

2. Morton Klass, *East Indians in Trinidad: A Study of Cultural Persistence* (New York and London: Columbia University Press, 1961).

3. V. S. Naipaul, "Prologue to an Autobiography," *Vanity Fair* 46, no. 2 (April 1983).

4. Naipaul, p. 138.

5. Eugene Goodheart, "Naipaul and the Voices of Negation," *Salmagundi* no. 54 (Fall 1981): 56.

6. Naipaul, pp. 54–58.

7. G. Jean-Aubry, *Joseph Conrad: Life and Letters* (Garden City, New York: Doubleday, Page and Company, 1927), p. 13.

English Poetry 1900–1950:
An Assessment

The author of this assessment declares at the start that literary history is "very rarely what contemporaries imagine it to be," and he proceeds to allot praise or blame with little regard for established opinions. There is a principle behind his views—he is interested in innovation; he believes that the "indubitable rhythm of the twentieth century" is "a language free from pretension as from any effort to be 'poetical,' words that follow speech so closely that the reader is hardly aware that he has not merely overheard the sentence." "But," he adds, "any rubbish will not do; the lines have the weight of long experience and digested thought."

C. H. Sisson's view of modern poetry in English is entirely personal; he makes no pretense of objectivity. English poetry, he says, includes any poetry written in English. He therefore admits the Scottish, Irish, and Welsh, as well as two Americans, Ezra Pound and T. S. Eliot. But there are surprising exclusions. Dylan Thomas is discussed, but not David Jones. Louis MacNeice and Austin Clarke are excluded. One could go on listing names. Edith Sitwell is dismissed—fair enough; her poetry was inferior to her publicity. But Robert Frost lived

This review of *English Poetry 1900–1950: An Assessment* by C. H. Sisson appeared in the *New York Times Book Review,* July 15, 1984. Copyright © 1984 by The New York Times Company. Reprinted by permission.

in England, and Mr. Sisson could scarcely be unaware of his existence—Frost may be said to have turned Edward Thomas into a poet.

Mr. Sisson is providing an assessment, not a survey. If we take the book this way it has a great deal to offer—the discovery of good poets who have been neglected and new views of those who are well known. He begins with A. H. Bullen who wrote at the turn of the century, a "lover of hedgerows," free, says Mr. Sisson, from "any suspicion of fashion," who wrote without pretensions to the poetic. "It could not be said that he did not speak out before he died, and that is all that anybody can do." Speaking out is another of Mr. Sisson's touchstones. The verse by Bullen that elicits his praise was of this kind: "Be wary; practice incredulity / Which makes the soul subtle and sinewy."

Thomas Hardy and W. B. Yeats began writing in the late nineteenth century and continued well into the twentieth. It is instructive to compare Mr. Sisson's treatment of these figures. Hardy's achievement, "the sheer bulk of closely-felt impressions, covering sixty years or more of his writing life, is without parallel in our literature." Hardy's very awkwardnesses are a virtue, "like a particular lurch or other movement which is habitual to some bodies." The rhythm of Hardy's verse is the rhythm of thought. Mr. Sisson even finds good things to say about *The Dynasts*, Hardy's magnum opus about the Napoleonic wars which few readers, certainly on this side the Atlantic, can have plowed through. The blank verse in *The Dynasts*, Mr. Sisson thinks, is "saved by its very flatness, for he is pretending to nothing that he does not mean to say." Hardy's lack of pretension is his profoundest contribution to the literature of the twentieth century.

Yeats, on the other hand, is pretentious. Though many have taken him at his own evaluation, Mr. Sisson has a different view. He thinks Yeats's "moralism" makes him Victorian rather than modern, and he gives Yeats's egotism short shrift. Yeats is "cut off from any fruitful tradition—from Swift, Berkeley and Burke . . . by the frivolous attitude to Christianity exhibited in 'The Mother of God' and in the references to von Hügel." There is worse. At moments Yeats "seems to approximate rather to the Marquis de Sade, whose not very profound, and perhaps insane, view was that the first duty of women was to lay themselves open to whatever lusts he chose to exercise upon them." Mr. Sisson's admiration of Yeats, such as it is, rests on the early poems, which have a languid charm, and those later in which Yeats casts aside pretense and conveys an impression of experience. The accent of truth is in the lines, "O who could have foretold / That the heart grows old?" Too often Yeats is cutting a figure, or there is a "parade of conventional conceptions," as in "Meditations in Time of Civil War" where he broods on the great houses that "helped him to build up his grandiose conception of himself" or which serve as a symbol for his "isolation from inferior persons."

There is a great deal of value, I believe, in reassessments such as this. In the United States we are exposed to much academic criticism—sometimes one wonders if there is any other—in which a few large figures are praised to the skies, their least writings tediously explained until the authors and their works seem unapproachable, the criticism standing between ourselves and any fresh reading of the material. We need very much to have critics such as Mr. Sisson, with his fearless views, if so-called "major" authors are to be read with enjoyment and understanding.

Mr. Sisson brings forward some poets of whom one has never heard—Edgell Rickword, for example, who wrote in the mid-1920s. He wrote about the Great War, "a few necrophilous poems, which are like nobody else's and which combine recollections of the trenches with a rather sinister eroticism." He wrote, for example, about the moon rising over the battlefield:

> Then I thought, standing in the ruined trench,
> (all round, dead Boche white-shirted lay like sheep),
> "Why does this damned entrancing bitch
> seek lovers only among them that sleep?"

Rickword also wrote in a Baudelairean manner about the "crowded, lust-ridden streets of London." It is not possible, of course, to claim that Rickword deserves as much attention for his war poetry as Wilfred Owen for his, or that Rickword's London is as memorable as the city in Eliot's *The Waste Land.* But the writings of "minor" authors are not dispensable. Poetry is valuable wherever it is found, and Rickword's pint is poetry as well as Eliot's gallon. Moreover, by concentrating exclusively on "major" authors, American critics exaggerate the originality of those authors and have no understanding of their place in a culture.

Once when I was driving toward the Welsh border the name Wenlock appeared on the road map. I quoted some lines by A. E. Housman to an American friend who was driving with me. He had never heard of Housman. And this was a professor of English in an American university! Many of our scholars know very little outside the figures they have been blinkered toward. They are not educated in any real sense.

Mr. Sisson's reassessments of major figures are as useful as his inclusions of neglected names. He considers Eliot's "Sweeney Agonistes" original and unique—in the poem Eliot dealt with common life as nowhere else in his verse—"the very rhythms show an openness to the draughts of the great world." On the other hand, Mr. Sisson does not share the general admiration for *Four Quartets.* The poetry is concocted, he thinks; the style of discourse "does not convince us as poetic apprehension of something hitherto undiscovered. It is *not* a raid on the 'inarticulate' but the articulation of an idea consciously accepted." Yes, that is the difference between *The Waste Land* and *Four Quartets,* and I think ability to see the difference is a measure of one's ability to appreciate poetry.

Mr. Sisson considers Pound's "Hugh Selwyn Mauberley" one of the essential poems of the century, and the *Cantos* are a "great treasure-trove," though the treasures are not equally valuable on every page. Pound's usury is a "noble subject" and perhaps the only possible one for a long poem in our age. Mr. Sisson is one of the critics who don't think Pound's support of Hitler and Mussolini worth discussing; he merely remarks that in Pisa "the United States military authorities incarcerated the sixty-year-old poet in a cage on a suspicion of treason." Some suspicion!

Mr. Sisson is a Wyndham Lewis enthusiast. There couldn't be many. Even if we concede that Lewis's "One-Way Song" is "the most subtle piece of argumentation put into English verse in the twentieth century," arguing in verse seems a bit foolish. Whom are you hoping to convince? In any case, when the occasion fades, so does the argument. Moreover, rhyming couplets and fourteen-syllable lines do not strike me as the "contribution to literary innovation" Mr. Sisson is looking for.

His opinion of W. H. Auden is likely to distress Auden's followers. According to Mr. Sisson, Auden began with an explosion, settled into a public voice with "Look, Stranger!" but after Auden came to the United States, "those interested simply in his contribution to literary innovation may stop."

No American critic would write a book as quirky and interesting as this. Mr. Sisson isn't afraid to say what he thinks. He isn't looking over his shoulder at an establishment as he writes. He isn't using the most recently approved critical method, just the intelligence that Eliot said was the only method.

On finishing the book one would like to have a satisfying quarrel with the author, then buy him a drink. If Pound and Eliot are admitted, where is William Carlos Williams, master of the kind of verse closely related to speech and based in experience that Mr. Sisson wants? But rather than complain about what is missing in Mr. Sisson's view of poetry in the twentieth century, I shall be grateful for what he has given us: an assessment of Edward Thomas as "one of the most profound poets of the century"; praise of Patrick Kavanagh's "The Great Hunger" that could induce readers to discover this remarkable narrative poem; praise of Hugh MacDiarmid, one of the great, neglected poets. Surely there have been enough books about Yeats, Pound, Eliot, and even Williams. It is time to put aside the views of the establishment, as this critic has done, and read poetry wherever it is found, flourishing in the byways.

III

The Act of Writing

"Chocolates"

"Chocolates"

Once some people were visiting Chekhov.
While they made remarks about his genius
the Master fidgeted. Finally
he said, "Do you like chocolates?"

They were astonished, and silent.
He repeated the question,
whereupon one lady plucked up her courage
and murmured shyly, "Yes."

"Tell me," he said, leaning forward,
light glinting from his spectacles,
"what kind? The light, sweet chocolate
or the dark, bitter kind?"

The conversation became general.
They spoke of cherry centers,
of almonds and Brazil nuts.
Losing their inhibitions
they interrupted one another.
For people may not know what they think
about politics in the Balkans,
or the vexed question of men and women,

but everyone has a definite opinion
about the flavor of shredded coconut.

"Chocolates" was published in *Caviare at the Funeral* (New York: Franklin Watts, 1980). The essay that follows was written at the request of Alberta Turner for *Forty-Five Contemporary Poets: The Creative Process,* edited by Alberta T. Turner (New York: Longman, 1985). Copyright © 1985 by Longman Inc.

Finally someone spoke of chocolates filled with liqueur,
and everyone, even the author of *Uncle Vanya,*
was at a loss for words.

As they were leaving he stood by the door
and took their hands.
                        In the coach returning to Petersburg
they agreed that it had been a most
unusual conversation.

The poem is based on an actual incident. Some women who
admired Chekhov paid him a visit. They wanted to talk about
his writing, but Chekhov, who probably welcomed the inter-
ruption of his work, said to one of them, "Do you like chocolates?" What followed was pretty much as I have it, though I
don't know if Chekhov stood by the door and took their
hands as they left—I have imagined his doing so, like a character in one of his plays.

The reader will have noticed a difference between this account and my poem. Chekhov's visitors were women—in the
poem they are "some people." I had to make this change, for
if I had said they were women it might have appeared that
Chekhov was condescending to women, talking about a frivolous subject, chocolates, because he thought women were not
to be taken seriously. Nothing, of course, could have been
further from Chekhov's mind—no one who has read
Chekhov could accuse him of holding women in contempt.
But there are always those who misunderstand, so I protected
Chekhov, and myself, against the charge by changing "wom-
en" to "some people." Of course, if a reader wishes to be
aggrieved he, or she, can always find a reason.

Reactions to the poem have been very favorable. I recall a
letter in the London *Times* praising "Chocolates" because, the
letter-writer said, it showed that poetry could be understood.
And audiences at poetry readings seem to understand: they
laugh at the line, "They spoke of cherry centers"—from relief—this is not going to be a serious poem—and laugh again
at the lines about shredded coconut and chocolates filled with

liqueur. Audiences at poetry readings are grateful for poetry that is at all entertaining—most poetry is deadly dull. They make appreciative noises at the words "*unusual* conversation," right at the end.

"Chocolates" is more serious than some of these listeners think. Superficially it may appear that I am poking fun at the kind of people who would go to see a famous author, but readers who feel superior to these visitors are missing the point. In real life I might find such people absurd but I would not hold them up to ridicule in a poem—I am more intelligent when I write than I am in person. The desire to see and speak to a great man or woman is not something to poke fun at. Only snobs, who are usually people of no talent, look down at those who have a sincere wish to better themselves.

Then what is the poem about? It is about happiness . . . the things that make people happy, and the delight we feel when we are able to express our happiness to another person. This may be the closest we get to heaven. Chekhov knew that people have preferences, though they may not be aware that they have them and may think that they should talk about philosophy instead. As Schopenhauer pointed out, we live according to our instincts and fashion our ideas accordingly—not the other way round, as Plato has it. A taste for chocolates may run deep—deeper than the wish to discuss *The Cherry Orchard* or politics in the Balkans.

And yet, though they like chocolates, people will talk about the things they think are expected. How boring for everyone!

This was why Chekhov brought up the subject of chocolates. It didn't have to be chocolates—anything they liked would have done . . . birthdays, for instance, or picnics . . . but chocolates were a happy choice. The visitors were relieved—like the audience at a poetry reading when the solemnity is broken. The visitors gave their opinions, tentatively at first, then in a torrent, "interrupting one another." This was what Chekhov wanted, to have them express their enthusiasm. It is the conversation that matters, not the subject.

What happened that day was nothing grand—nothing as

holy as what might have taken place in Tolstoy's house, but far more enjoyable all around.

Chekhov's poems and stories are about people who are prevented by character or circumstance from being happy. "My holy of holies," Chekhov said, "is the human body, health, intelligence, talent, inspiration, love and the most absolute freedom—freedom from violence and lying, whatever forms they may take."

So he asked his visitors to tell him if they liked chocolates, and when they said they did, the barriers were broken down. What followed was a communion of souls, and as they were talking about something they liked it was a happy communion.

Writers like Chekhov—but is there any writer like Chekhov?—through their sympathy and humor show that it is possible to live in the world. There is poverty, sickness, and old age. There is bureaucracy. . . . Still, we can understand and love one another. Since the world will never be any different from what it is—not as long as it is inhabited by human beings—Chekhov's is the ultimate wisdom.

About the writing of "Chocolates"* . . .

I had heard this story about Chekhov some years before I wrote the poem.

I was staying at a friend's house in the country. On Sunday he and his wife went to church, and I didn't feel like going. I was left behind with the *New York Times* and the *Boston Globe*. Perhaps "Chocolates" was triggered by something he and I had been talking about, some remark about poetry . . . I don't recall. I picked up my notebook and started writing. The poem was written in a few minutes. I may have changed one or two words afterwards, or changed a line-break, but nothing important.

"This poem," one reader observes, "generally uses the

---

*The editor (Alberta Turner) had mentioned certain aspects of the writing of "Chocolates" that I might wish to discuss. The following remarks were an attempt to answer her questions.

rhythms, syntax, and diction of prose fiction." I don't think so—to my ear the poem moves in lines of verse. If "Chocolates" were printed not in lines but as prose, the reader would soon be aware that lines of verse were struggling to break free.

(Incidentally, I have a low opinion of prose poems, unless they are written by Baudelaire. They don't have the absolute rhythm that you get from lines of verse; the rhythms are arbitrary, and so the work as a whole falls short of poetry. Poetry is absolute—it could not be other than it is. The "prose poem" could be written several different ways and the effect would be more or less the same. Prose may be very well written, of course, but it can never have the power of poetry written in lines.)

Are the syntax and diction of verse different from the syntax and diction of prose? I don't think so. A long time ago Ezra Pound remarked that poetry must be as well written as prose. That is to say, verse must sound as though the writer meant it. Verse is not a convention of style but an expression of mind. If the language of verse differs from prose it is not because the style was fetched from a distance but because verse is more highly charged with meaning, requiring more complex expression.

All good writing is experimental, but readers are listening for the rhythms and diction of poems they already know, so a new kind of poetry is said to be "antipoetic." Wordsworth in his time was said to be writing prose. So were Whitman, Frost, Eliot, and, of course, William Carlos Williams.

For twenty years I have been developing a kind of writing in verse that would accommodate my thoughts as easily as prose yet have a lyric flow. Coleridge said that the poet "diffuses a tone and spirit of unity, that blends, and (as it were) *fuses,* each into each, by that synthetic and magical power, to which we have exclusively appropriated the name of imagination." In poems such as "Chocolates" I have attempted to enter into a situation and imagine it strongly so that everything—words, phrases, and sentences—would fall into place with no seeming effort on my part.

The Terms of Life Itself:
Writing "Quiet Desperation"

Quiet Desperation

At the post office he sees Joe McInnes.
Joe says, "We're having some people over.
It'll be informal. Come as you are."

She is in the middle
of preparing dinner. Tonight
she is trying an experiment:
Hal Burgonyaual—Fish-Potato Casserole.
She has cooked and drained the potatoes
and cut the fish in pieces.
Now she has to "mash potatoes,
add butter and hot milk," et cetera.

He relays Joe's invitation.
"No," she says, "not on your life.
Muriel McInnes is no friend of mine."

It appears that she told Muriel
that the Goldins live above their means,
and Muriel told Mary Goldin.

He listens carefully, to get things right.
The feud between the Andersons and the Kellys

"Quiet Desperation" was published in *The Best Hour of the Night* (New York: Ticknor and Fields, 1983). "The Terms of Life Itself: Writing 'Quiet Desperation'" originally appeared in *Singular Voices* (New York: Avon Books, 1985), edited by Stephen Berg.

began with Ruth Anderson calling Mike Kelly
a reckless driver. Finally
the Andersons had to sell their house and move.

Social life is no joke.
It can be the only life there is.

*

In the living room the battle of Iwo Jima
is in progress, watched by his son.
Men are dying on the beach,
pinned down by a machine gun.

The marine carrying the satchel charge
falls. Then Sergeant Stryker
picks up the charge and starts running.

Now you are with the enemy machine gun
firing out of the pillbox
as Stryker comes running,
bullets at his heels kicking up dust.
He makes it to the base of the pillbox,
lights the charge, raises up,
and heaves it through the opening.
The pillbox explodes . . .
the NCO's wave, "Move out!"

And he rises to his feet.
He's seen the movie. Stryker gets killed
just as they're raising the flag.

*

A feeling of pressure . . .
There is something that needs to be done
immediately.

           But there is nothing,
only himself. His life is passing,
and afterwards there will be eternity,
silence, and infinite space.

He thinks, "Firewood!"—
and goes to the basement,
takes the Swede-saw off the wall,
and goes outside, to the woodpile.

He carries an armful to the sawhorse
and saws the logs into smaller pieces.
In twenty minutes he has a pile of firewood
cut just the right length.
He carries the cut logs into the house
and arranges them in a neat pile
next to the fireplace.

Then looks around for something else to do,
to relieve the feeling of pressure.

The dog!
He will take the dog for a walk.

*

They make a futile procession . . .
he commanding her to "Heel!"—
she dragging back or straining ahead.

The leaves are turning yellow.
Between the trunks of the trees
the cove is blue, with ripples.
The swans—this year there are seven—
are sailing line astern.

But when you come closer
the rocks above the shore are littered
with daggers of broken glass
where the boys sat on summer nights
and broke beer bottles afterwards.

And the beach is littered, with cans,
containers, heaps of garbage,
newspaper wadded against the sea-wall.
Someone has even dumped a mattress . . .
a definite success!
Some daring guy, some Stryker
in the pickup speeding away.

He cannot bear the sun
going over and going down . . .
the trees and houses vanishing
in quiet every day.

The ideas that make a poem present themselves as images. Their significance may not immediately be apparent and indeed may never be. But poetry does not wait on meaning, and certain things insist on being noticed, at times with the power of hallucinations. When I wrote "Quiet Desperation" the scenery was already in place, the situations familiar: a woman looking at a recipe as she prepared dinner; television going in the living room; sawing some wood for the fireplace; walking down to the water. There were houses overlooking the road, a screen of trees, and everything seemed to drowse in a sea light.

But poetry is more than description, just as a living creature is more than the sum of its parts. Poetry is a drama in which objects are cut loose from their moorings and sent flying to make their own connections. The first step, therefore, was to get my controlling mind out of the poem and treat the subject impersonally. So I embodied my ideas in a narrative—there would be a character to do the observing, and one or two others. The method isn't infallible—a particularly obstreperous ego will struggle not to let go, but writing about people in a narrative turns the poem away from the self and compels it to face the world.

I sent the man in the poem to the post office where he met a man named McInnes who invited him to his house. I brought my character home and gave him a wife. They had a conversation in which she rejected McInnes's invitation, and this gave me an opportunity to express my own feelings about the narrowness of small-town life. Not only in small towns . . . the problem of how to get along with people sociably is universal. I write about a small town because in order to write with conviction I must have a place in mind, and this is a setting I know—it is where I live.

I had the man go into the living room, and gave him a son who was watching John Wayne on television capture the island of Iwo Jima. I enjoyed putting in the details, especially "bullets at his heels kicking up dust." This is what machine gun bullets do in movies. I like putting into a poem things people accept as true—it is the pleasure Flaubert got from quoting "received ideas." If you want to write poetry about people you must put in what they think, not just your own feelings and opinions. Novelists know this, but these days few poets seem to—they have little interest in the thoughts and feelings of others. This makes for poetry with no observed life in it and, of course, no humor.

When I put in John Wayne on Iwo Jima I had no idea how this would tie in, but you have to let things happen and trust there will be a connection. The more the poem seems to be writing itself, the more joy you take in it. And if you can bring it off, if the connections are there, you have a real poem, one that lives and breathes by itself.

This is writing by impulse, and I know no other way in which good poetry can be written. But you must be able to trust the poem and withstand frustration. For the impulse may flag and the poem cease to move. When this happens the writer may try to forge ahead by sheer will, to think of something, to invent. . . . Many poems are written in this way, and the results are not good. They may look like poems but they are only exercises—they don't make you feel that they had to be written.

I had come to such a place—could not see where the poem was going. But instead of trying to make up something I put what I was feeling into the poem—my frustration.

Wordsworth said that poetry takes its origin from emotion recollected in tranquility. Readers have concentrated on the recollecting but the phrase "takes its origin" is just as important. The act of writing begins with memory but is different from mere recollection—it is a reconstruction of experience with something added, the plus being the emotion of the poet as he writes. The emotion that creates a poem is not the emotion you had when you were having the experience, but the emotion you are having now, as you write.

If you write out of impulse, as I have said, it may leave you suddenly. Then,

As high as we have mounted in delight
In our dejection do we sink as low . . .

And now I was dejected and the poem was sinking. And still there was a pressure to write. I felt a kind of desperation.

This was what I put into the poem—I made the character feel my own desperation. Putting this feeling into the poem made it more than a description and gave it such depth and meaning as it has. It brought the character to life and made him interesting—to myself and, it has seemed, to others.

Many have known the dread that can come upon you suddenly, a cloud blotting out the sun. You are aware that life is passing, "and afterwards there will be eternity, / silence, and infinite space." Your pulse is racing and you feel a need to act, to stave off some disaster.

I once remarked in a poem that I could never think of anything to make my characters do. I meant this as irony, but a critic took it to be an admission of failure. When you are writing out of feeling you don't have to make anything happen—the writing is interesting and the characters are alive, like Hamlet, though they are standing still. On the other hand, if feeling is absent no amount of plotting helps. The writing and incidents will not move.

In "Quiet Desperation" form follows feeling. The third part begins with "A feeling of pressure. . . ." The sentence fragment and short line suggest that the pressure is overwhelming. A longer line follows:

There is something that needs to be done

The next line consists of one word, "immediately." This is urgent and peremptory. Then there is a step down, the poem continuing to the right of the page. The form sags as the feeling sags:

But there is nothing,
only himself.

There follows the reflection about eternity with its echo of Pascal. Then the thinker pulls himself together and acts, the short brisk lines evoking decisive action:

> He thinks, "Firewood!"
> and goes to the basement . . .

Having given my own anxiety to the character I knew what he would do . . . saw firewood, walk the dog . . . things I had done myself on such occasions. Anything to relieve the pressure.

He is walking past the slopes and woods of the landscape celebrated by William Sidney Mount a hundred years ago in his paintings of Long Island. As he walks he looks at the trees and grass and the cove glimpsed through the trees. Nature is beautiful.

But when he gets down to the shore he finds that garbage has been dumped on the natural scene. There are daggers of broken glass on the rocks. At this point I discover the relevance of the battle of Iwo Jima. In a time of war the young men who smash bottles and strew garbage would be heroes. They have no education to speak of—our public schools have seen to that. They cannot sit still and think. But they are full of energy, so they get drunk and smash bottles. Or perhaps try a bit of burglary . . . anything to break the monotony of their lives. If there was a war they would go to it.

Not only in the States . . . millions of people all over the world are suffering from boredom and what Baudelaire called "spleen," a feeling of frustration, a rage at conditions, at the terms of life itself.

Deprived of the opportunity to lead a company of marines, Sergeant Stryker dumps a mattress on the beach and speeds away in his pickup. It is a small victory over the forces of law and boredom. Sergeant Stryker needs a war to keep him going. He cannot stand the monotony of peace and the feeling that his life is being spent to no purpose. But this is what life is—it is banal, and the rewards are fleeting. If we wish to live we must learn to withstand the banality.

My own solution is to write a poem—others will have other solutions.

What there is to say about the form and style of the poem may be said in a few words. The stresses within the lines are so variable that I would not call them feet. I do observe, however, a preponderance of lines with three or four stresses. The lines vary in length, and I pause at the end of the line or run on as I would if I were speaking. This kind of verse isn't entirely free and it isn't written in meter. The term I think best describes it is "free form."

Writing in 1844, Emerson said, "It is not metres, but a metre-making argument that makes a poem—a thought so passionate and alive that like the spirit of a plant or an animal it has an architecture of its own, and adorns nature with a new thing."

"Quiet Desperation" has "architecture," to use Emerson's word. The lines have marked rhythms and a form, not predetermined but rising from the matter in hand. The term "free form" describes this kind of writing more accurately than "free verse," which suggests an absence of form of any kind.

The voice of poetry is not the voice in which you say good morning or talk to the man who fills your gas tank—still, there is a connection. I agree with Wordsworth that poetry should be a selection—with the word *selection* emphasized—of the language people actually use. I listen as I write for the sounds of speech.

There are readers who want the images in a poem to be farfetched, things we have not seen or heard. Others want a style that draws attention to itself. And there are those who estimate the value of a poet in direct proportion to his unwillingness or failure to make sense. For such readers my writing can hold little interest—I write about feelings people share, in language that can be understood.

Off the Cuff

Do you go back and rewrite your early poems?

After it's been published, I never touch it, except maybe move a comma. I don't believe in the business of rewriting old poems because I think that means you have an idea of yourself you're trying to impose. There are some exceptions, but in general, I think you wind up with something which is not true to what you were then or what you are now. I'd rather write a new poem.

Reading The Best Hour, *one comes away with a strong sense of storyline and characters. This brings to mind that you started as a fiction writer and had a few stories and a novel published.*

I didn't really start as a fiction writer. I hoped to be one, but I was no good at it. I'm still no good at it. My latest failure was only three years ago. But, I do work in narrative with poetry; for some reason my imagination only works in narrative. When I start telling a story, it builds up with layers. I have the action, and beyond it there are layers of meanings that come into it, and that makes a poem for me. The bare action is not enough. Once I've begun a story, all sorts of cross-references start to happen, start to echo against each other, until finally it has the feeling of a poem.

This interview first appeared in the *Minetta Review* 3 (New York University, 1983–84). The interviewer was Edith Keller.

In The Best Hour, *quotidian activities are turned into poetry. One almost wants to state that what you do in your poetry, Raymond Carver does in his fiction.*

Yes. And it's curious. He sent me his book a couple of years ago, and when I read his stories I said to myself, God, this is like my poems. It's the same kind of story he's telling. A bit off. I can't write about the "normal" because I'm immersed in it. I feel I have to get a bit away from life to write about it. So, in order to make some comment, I choose characters who are a little outside life. Quite often my characters are based on someone I've once met, but I do a tremendous amount of changing, moving them from one country to another, and so on. It's very hard to know what's going to set you off on a story-poem; it could be a person you met for ten minutes, but something in that person triggered your imagination. On the other hand, I can't write about my next-door neighbors; not because I'm afraid to, but simply because my imagination hasn't been triggered by them.

Asimov once described his method of working. He sits at his typewriter and begins to type whatever comes to his mind, and then something happens, a form develops.

That's the best way to do it. You see, there is a mistake many beginning writers, many students make. They think they have to have a clear idea in their head in order to write. But this is not so. A preconceived idea is not necessarily the best idea to write from at all. You have to discover it. The excitement in a piece of writing is the excitement the author felt as he was discovering what was going to happen next. There are poets who write essays; they have a preconceived idea and they sit down and write it out, and that makes, I think, dead poetry. A lot of the *New Yorker* poetry is like that.

When do you know that you have a poem?

Excitement. I push things around until they start to excite me, little blocks of experience, images. I push them around and they start to relate to each other. It begins to move, and it grips you, it takes you along with it, and then you just know, you feel it's moving, and all the elements are there, the rhythm, the sound, the movement.

In your poem, "Quiet Desperation," the man is suddenly seized with

> *A feeling of pressure . . .*
> *There is something that needs to be done immediately.*
> *But there is nothing, only himself.*

This pressure, is it the pressure to write?

No, that was a different kind of pressure I was describing there; it was panic, which I get sometimes, and I suppose other people get it too. It's unfocused anxiety. You suddenly realize you're getting old, that you're alone in the universe, that between you and space there is nothing, and your pulse starts to accelerate for no reason really. It's like what Pascal said. The silence of those infinite spaces terrifies me.

The pressure to write is different. You see, I get up in the morning and I go to my typewriter. And I sit there. I don't try to write when I don't feel like it, but I do go to my study and put myself in a place where I can work. When I work on a book of prose I write every day, whether I like it or not. With poetry I have to wait until a new wave of images, feelings, accumulates in me. Then I get itchy and go to the typewriter and haunt it. This pressure is a kind of feeling of gears moving in your head, and words and ideas, and why am I not writing? You have a feeling the machine is ready to go, but is not gripping on anything. It's like a machine with the wheels spinning, but not gripping. And you feel the pressure to go to the typewriter because those wheels should hit something.

In your poem, "The Previous Tenant," you touch on the subtle suburbanite anti-Semitism.

Oh yes. It wasn't directed at me in so many words, but it's all around me where I live. There's an area in Port Jefferson called Belle Terre, and I think that up to about twenty-five years ago, Jews were just not allowed there. Now Jews live there, but I think that black people are still not welcome. There's a great deal of racism of one kind or another in the suburbs. The so-called upper classes—they think they are upper class—they have their jokes and so on. But it's not only them. I was reading this book about Wallace Stevens. He was an anti-Semite, and he disliked black people. He took his family to a restaurant one day and came right out again and said, "There are too many Jews in there." That's Wallace Stevens. Isn't that a beauty. Thank God I never had to meet that man.

I may be old-fashioned; I thought racism would phase out by now, but it doesn't seem to be happening. I think that if black and white children were brought up together, this could change. I went to a school of mixed blacks and whites in the West Indies, and there was no racism in my school. Education is the key, but education is tied in with economics, and the economic situation is not allowing it to happen.

Do you have an "ideal reader" in your mind?

Yes. My reader is someone who is not affected. Someone who is intelligent and has a pretty good emotional response; immediate and direct. My poems are available. I don't write for the self-proclaimed intellectual, for someone who says, for example, I can't understand John Ashbery, but he's a wonderful poet; I don't write for that kind of person.

As you say, your poems are available. You don't use allusions to mythology, for instance, while there are people who would tell you it's a must.

That's clutter. That's all clutter. Bric-a-brac. It's like a living room stuffed with furniture. It has nothing to do with poetry. It's cultural clutter. And this is the tragedy of the present situation. We have these people like Brodsky, to name one, and Helen Vendler, who isn't even a poet, misguiding the young. Brodsky is coming out with these statements these days, saying that all American poets owe a great debt to Auden. This is absolute nonsense, but the point is, young people listen to these men and women who hold positions of academic power, and they think it's true. While the real poets in America don't waste their time answering these kinds of assertions. The poets of real talent, people like Snyder, Levertov, Duncan, all these people are busy writing poems, living and thinking very deeply. They don't have the time for this chit-chat. The literary scene in New York right now is in the hands of people like Brodsky. It's all political; they give each other prizes. There was a picture of the whole gang of them in the *New York Times* the other day.

How does one fight something like that?

The best way to do it is write your own poems. The best literary criticism is writing your own poems. It doesn't matter what certain people say about poetry. You see what's happening: we have these people, a handful of poets and critics, running the Academy of American Poets, coming out with these statements on what poetry is or should be. But they know where other poets stand, what other poets think of them. That's why they stick so close together.

Some time ago you said that poetry is of no importance in the United States.

Yes, and I still feel this way. Poetry doesn't have real importance here; it can't affect our policy in any way, it doesn't affect the public. Poetry is of no national importance, is what I meant. In other countries, Russia for example, or Latin America, the poets are figures of importance on the scene. It just doesn't fit with American life. We are not a reading, imaginative reading, nation. We can read manuals. It goes back to the fact that our civilization here was built by practical men. A good poet in the U.S. can expect to sell about three thousand copies of his book, whereas in the Scandinavian countries, for example, a book of poetry will sell twenty thousand copies.

Quite often when there is a political wave, it produces the kind of poetry that addresses itself to political situations, and people go to a poetry reading as if it were a political meeting. How much it has to do with the love of poetry is another question. Poetry itself doesn't have a large audience, but you don't really need it. You must feel you have readers, listeners; that's important. But you don't need a great number.

What is your guiding principle when you conduct a poetry workshop?

I assume a poem has an ideal shape, but I don't impose my idea on a student. I try to see what kind of poem each student wants to write, and I help him in that direction. There's no use telling a student to write a different kind of poem from what he wants to do; that's terrible, that's destructive. It's more like saying, if that's the kind of poem you want to write, then you'd better learn to do it well, and I push the student to not settle for any easy solution. Mainly, you must work within the terms of what the student is trying to do.

And one last question. You once said that we are all beginners when starting a new poem. As an advanced beginner, do you have a word of advice for the beginner-student poet?

Read. Read as many poets as you can. Read until your head is filled with words, images, and rhythms.

Giving Up

Wordsworth said that poetry takes its origin from emotion recollected in tranquility. This has been misread to mean that poetry is recollection. But though poetry may originate in memory it is creation—*poema,* a made thing. The excitement we feel when we read a poem is the excitement the poet felt in the act of writing.

Charles Olson put it in a nutshell: "Art does not seek to describe but to enact."

According to Olson there is an interaction between objects and the mind of the poet, who is himself an object. Out of this "act in the . . . field of objects" comes the impulse to write, "the head, by way of the ear, to the syllable, the heart, by way of the breath, to the line." These connections strike me as pure Rube Goldberg. I shall be told they are figures of speech and not to be taken literally. Very well, then why use them at all? It is merely confusing.

But Olson is right on target when he says that the style, structure, and meaning of the poem are determined in the act of writing. What follows is an attempt to show how tides of thought and feeling, as one writes, bring poetry into being, or cause it to stop.

Once in Italy I wrestled with a poem I thought I had to write. I was living at the time on Lake Como, and the view of the shore from my window, the blue of the lake, the Alps on

---

Written at the request of Michael Cuddihy and published in *Ironwood* 24 (Fall 1984), edited by Michael Cuddihy.

the far side, seemed to require a response. What kind of writer was I, if I could not write about this?

I walked down to the village and looked at the shops, the people, the *Ghisallo* or *Narciso* coming in to dock. There was a swimming pool at the Grand Hotel; I went there to swim and look at the tourists sunning themselves in deck chairs.

> A girl browned by the sun,
> nipples like heavy bronze coins.
> Her husband leans close . . .
> long, black eyelashes,
> whispering . . .

The breasts of the women were exposed. For an American this took some getting used to. I wrote some acrimonious lines about these people, describing the men as having weak limbs and soft bellies, the women as scatterbrained. One, whom I called a "faded blonde," was reading *L'Espresso*. "Et tu, che specie di amante sei?" said the cover. "And you, what kind of lovers are you?" I framed an answer to the question, replying that I was

> A lover of the mountain,
> of peaks flushed with rose . . .

It was a thoroughly sanctimonious performance. I was finding fault with people's behavior because I had no poetic energy. Poets are said to be irascible—I think they are likely to become so when they cannot write.

At the same time that I was trying to write this poem, I was trying to write another based on an incident I had read about in the *Letters* of Pliny the Younger. In 79 A.D. his uncle the naturalist sailed to Vesuvius to observe the volcano in eruption, and was asphyxiated. I retold the story in lines of verse.

> Hot stones and ashes were falling
> and the captain wanted to turn back,
> but he said, "Fortune befriends the brave,
> carry me to Pompionanus!"

But what was the use of turning Pliny's prose into verse? So I tried to graft the erupting volcano onto the scene at the Grand Hotel, in order to make a satirical point. While the idle rich are enjoying themselves a cloud is gathering, et cetera. I imagined that from where I sat I could see Pliny the Elder and his friends running down to the sea. He was a fat man and puffed as he ran; they were holding pillows over their heads for protection from the falling stones.

This is the kind of ironic juxtaposition one sees in a movie, but poetry should be more original. Though American poets have only two or three thousand readers—you can hardly call it a public—readers of poetry are more demanding than the aficionados of film.

With the poems separately, and the two grafted together, I had reached a dead end. Poetry may include satire but it should not stop there. Life is too complicated for such easy solutions.

The pleasure in writing comes of writing about what matters most to ourselves. But neither the scene by the pool at the Grand Hotel nor the eruption of Vesuvius was of any real concern to me. Yet I had felt compelled to write several drafts.

At this point I decided to give up. Poetry is a "spontaneous overflow" as Wordsworth said, or it is nothing—there is no pleasure in it for the poet and can be none for the reader.

In this relaxed mood—you could call it tranquility—I wrote a few lines that had no bearing on the subjects I had been trying to write about. I imagined that one of the villagers was speaking to me, pointing out that I was a tourist myself and therefore not serious. He was saying

> You walk around the village
> and buy the silk of Como that is famous
> and sit on a beach with the ladies . . .
> Signore, it isn't so strange,
> after all, that you cannot write.

The movement from the first-person voice to the voice of another enabled me to see myself clearly. I was a tourist with a wish to write. My deepest self lay hidden, the power that enables one to write poetry in abeyance, waiting for another time, another country perhaps.

Some time after I had returned to the United States I picked up the work sheets of the poems and looked them over. Then I wrote:

> You will never write the poem about Italy

and a poem began running from start to finish. The momentum gave the form. Form isn't made by hammering boards together and pouring concrete, though that is the way it is taught in some writing workshops. Form is the shape of an idea. The idea carries the poem or story from start to finish. A writer with an idea can do anything he likes and it will work—he can digress or make abrupt transitions, and his own interest in what he is saying will make them part of the story. If you don't have an idea, saw and hammer as you may, the structure creaks and leans sideways.

This is my quarrel with writing workshops: they concentrate on the boards and nails, trying to find a better word, changing a line-break, worrying at an image.

My quarrel with certain writers is that the ideas they express are not necessary. There are writers of verse who publish a new book every two or three years. Rilke wrote two elegies at Duino in 1912, and waited ten years to write the rest—but look at the result!

The line I had written, "You will never write the poem about Italy," gave the theme: poetry is not found in objects, it comes from within.

> What Socrates said about love
> is true of poetry—where is it?
> Not in beautiful faces and distant scenery
> but the one who writes and loves.
>
> In your life here on this street . . .

The idea formed sentences, line-breaks, and paragraphs. The paragraphs became stanzas, the rhythm creating the divisions. Within each stanza the lines varied in rhythm and length. Images arose effortlessly.

The speaker of the poem said that poetry was to be found in drab surroundings, and that you must observe your neighbors as they get up by the alarm clock, go to the train, and mount the station platform. You must watch as, "grasping briefcases," they

> pass beyond your gaze
> and hurl themselves into the flames.

I visualized the station platform as the parapet of a trench they mounted in order to launch themselves into the day's work, the world of business and industry. Lives are expended there as surely as in war. But a reader to whom I explained the process by which the poem came to be written, as I have explained it here, pointed out that I had got the eruption of Vesuvius into it after all.

The figure of Pliny the Elder, the "savant" as his nephew calls him in the old-fashioned Loeb translation, continued to appear. I saw him on board ship striking a pose: "Carry me to Pompionanus!" When he arrives at the villa of his friend he calls for a bath, then dines heartily, making cheerful conversation to allay the fears of the others. He sleeps through the night—the people lying outside the door can hear him snoring, because he is "pretty fat." He is asleep while Vesuvius thunders and the walls shake. Next morning he and his companions, "balancing reasons," decide it would be better outside than in, so they put pillows on their heads—"napkins" says the ridiculous translation—and run down to the shore. But the waves are too high for them to push off. Pliny lies down on a sail in order to rest. There is a smell of sulphur . . . supported by two slaves he struggles to rise . . . but falls back. The body is found some days later, appearing, says his nephew, like that of a man who is sleeping rather than one who has died. The letter doesn't mention what happened to the slaves.

The Younger Pliny's description of the erupting volcano— a cloud like a tree rising into the sky—evoked the nuclear explosions we have seen in pictures. Now, others may have a different view, but I think that, given the propensity of nations for settling their differences by force, we have not seen the last of nuclear warfare. If the nineteenth century was haunted by the specter of communism, the twentieth is haunted by the specter of annihilation.

How are we to think about this? On the one hand we must do all we can to prevent it. But suppose we cannot and the thing we fear comes to pass? I picked up the sheets of the poem I had failed to write. This time I had an idea.

Pliny owned two villas on Lake Como that he called "Comedy" and "Tragedy." I wrote about the events leading to his death and concluded:

> Was this Tragedy? I don't think
> that Pliny would have thought so,
> being a naturalist, caught up
> in the study of his subject,
> the volcano . . .

In both "The Unwritten Poem" and "The Naturalist and the Volcano" poetry attended on an idea: in the first instance, the idea that poetry can be found in ordinary surroundings and ordinary lives; in the second, that if we have a strong enough purpose, like Pliny's interest in science, we shall not be frightened about what will become of us.

I once said that "poetry does not wait on meaning." This is true: a rhythm may be felt, images may appear before we know what to make of them. A phrase may be heard by itself in isolation.

But the poem begins with an idea. Until there is one, scenes and images hold no interest. The idea must be one that really concerns us, and if we write about what we think and feel we may move others, for we are not so different one from another.

Irregular Impulses
Some Remarks on Free Verse

There is always some critic to say that free verse is not poetry, it is prose broken into lines.

In the old days readers of poetry knew what to expect: regular feet and rhymes. The reader could expect, in Wordsworth's description, "small, but continual and regular impulses of pleasurable surprise from the metrical arrangement."

But all that has changed. In the twentieth century we demand that the artist be original, and poetry is the expression of an individual rather than an exercise in a traditional literary form. In the middle of the nineteenth century Whitman wrote free verse, and twenty years later the Symbolist poets experimented with it. By the time of the First World War a number of poets had found that they could write more expressively in free verse. At the present time in the United States there is no longer a class that feels obliged to maintain traditional forms of literature; free verse is the commonest kind, and young poets scarcely write anything else.

"A poem," said Coleridge, "is that species of composition which is opposed to works of science by proposing for its *immediate* object pleasure, not truth; and from all other species (having this object in common with it) it is discriminated by proposing to itself such delight from the whole as is com-

This essay first appeared in the *Ohio Review,* no. 28 (Ohio University, 1982).

patible with a distinct gratification from each component part."

It is the structure of the poem that counts rather than its being written in meter or irregular lines. Verse in meter is not poetry unless it has the synthesizing power of imagination Coleridge speaks of, and irregular or free verse may be poetry of the highest kind.

But could not Coleridge's description apply just as accurately to some kinds of prose? Doesn't the total impression of Flaubert's *Un Coeur Simple* depend on the writing in every sentence, the phrasing, the images, the rhythm? Yes, but sentences are not lines. Verse is written in lines—this is what makes the difference.

In regular verse the line is perceived by the ear. So many feet, then we listen for the next line. The poet writing in regular meter gives the comfort that a child has in a rocking cradle. Even when he is dealing with obscure ideas or unpleasant situations he comforts you with "regular impulses of pleasurable surprise."

But the lines of free verse have to be seen—I mean literally, with your eyes. Then you perceive the rhythm. The essence of free verse, that which distinguishes it from regular verse as well as prose, is that the line is seen as a separate thing.

The free-verse poet compels you, by the unexpectedness of his writing, to pay close attention. You have to make sense of the words and see how the syllables are to be stressed. You cannot rely on what has gone before, a pattern established at the start. As Lawrence said, it is poetry of the present, the immediate flow of thought and feeling.

This is why some readers dislike it. Not only does free verse fail to provide a rocking motion, but it demands that they pay attention to every syllable. Where is the pleasure in that?

But in practice it is not difficult to read free verse. You have to get the hang of the poet's voice. It is not the language of speech—no poet writes as he speaks—but a thinking voice.

Regular verse can go on for some time without doing anything remarkable and still give the pleasure Wordsworth describes—the ear keeps listening for the chime. But with free verse as every line draws attention to itself it had better be interesting. Free verse makes for concentrated writing and short poems. Pound in the *Cantos,* Williams in *Paterson,* attempted to write an epic in free verse. But both works have stretches of sluggish or incoherent writing.

If we do not look for epics, there have been poems in free verse that sustain interest for several hundred lines—"The Great Hunger," for example, by the Irish poet Patrick Kavanagh. It runs to over eight hundred lines and, speaking for myself, I have never wanted a poem to be longer. Not unless the poet were Homer or Dante.

Kavanagh had a theme, the repression of sex that one finds among the people of Ireland. Having a theme enabled him to write at length, and he also had the ability to tell a story. Most American poets lack a theme. Their experience is limited to themselves—they have no sense of a community. If they write about society, they seem to have no part themselves in the life they are writing about. If they speak of "the people," it is for some political reason, and they do not write about the middle class for they despise it. After a while they are reduced to making casual remarks about matters of no importance.

But Kavanagh is at one with blundering humanity.

> O let us kneel where the blind ploughman kneels
> And learn to live without despairing
> In a mud-walled space—
> Illiterate, unknown and unknowing.
> Let us kneel where he kneels
> And feel what he feels.

In some passages Kavanagh uses meter and rhyme. For instance, when Patrick Maguire is sitting on a gate, singing to himself:

> Sitting on a wooden gate,
> Sitting on a wooden gate,

> Sitting on a wooden gate,
> He didn't care a damn.

Shakespeare mixed his iambic pentameters with short lines and passages of prose when the situation called for it, and there is no rule against the free-verse poet's using meter and rhyme when, as in this instance, it helps the story. The point about free verse is that it is free. You would expect, however, that the body of the poem would be in irregular lines, passages in meter and rhyme being the exception, and so it is in "The Great Hunger." The body of the poem is carried by an irregular, conversational line.

> The mother sickened and stayed in bed all day,
> Her head hardly dented the pillow, so light and thin it had
>   worn,
> But she still enquired after the household affairs.

Do these lines seem flat? Perhaps they do, but a long poem may have passages of lower intensity—in fact, a letting-down may be wanted in view of the poem as a whole. To write as Gerard Manley Hopkins and Dylan Thomas write, pounding every line, would not be the way to tell a story.

Some American poets have been reacting against free verse, or so I have been told. A poet visiting San Francisco has announced that free verse is dead. This is the kind of pronouncement poets make when they are giving readings of their own poetry. But in fact the shoe is on the other foot. If you were to put American poets who write free verse in one scale and poets who write regular forms in the other, the latter would fly up. Not only are they fewer in number—I mean those who have any merit at all—their writing tends to be light. In our time writing in regular form leads to writing light verse; the poet who writes in meter and rhyme reassures his reader that he need not take it seriously—it is only literature, *au fond* an amusement.

I have spoken of a thinking voice. The voice is individual—I do not see how it can be measured, though Williams spoke of a "variable foot." It depends on the patterns of speech, the physical makeup, the psyche of the individual. If the free-verse poet writes dull poems, it is not because he is not writing in rhyme and meter, but because he has nothing interesting to say, no structure and no style. Learning to write sonnets will not make him a better poet. Let him read Homer and Dante for a change—he needs to enlarge his imagination.

Of Language and Line-Breaks

Carruth, Simic, and Haines

Taking a specimen of free verse and printing it as prose, without the line-breaks, then arguing that, as the divisions into lines cannot be deduced from the language itself, they were never really necessary. . . You don't have to be a lawyer to know that there is something wrong with this method of arguing. The poet is charged with failing to do something that he never intended. What the poet intended was for the reader to see with his eyes, or hear with his ears, the divisions of the lines where they were placed, not for the reader to guess, from the order of the words alone, i.e., a prose paragraph, where the lines of verse would end. For writing to be

---

This first appeared in *Field,* no. 8 (Spring 1973), and was reprinted in *A Field Guide to Contemporary Poetry and Poetics,* edited by Stuart Friebert and David Young (New York: Longman, 1980).

Hayden Carruth had published an article in the *Hudson Review* in which he wrote out poems by Charles Simic and John Haines as prose paragraphs in order to show that the language was "inert" and the division in lines did not make it move as verse. He said that the line had ceased to function because the language had become "too dull to sustain the measure."

Provoked by Carruth's essay, Sandra McPherson wrote an essay, "The Working Line," which was published in *Field.* She said, "We write in lines because we plant a vegetable garden in rows, because we have ribs, because . . . "

The editors of *Field* asked James Wright and the author to comment on the McPherson essay.

read as lines of verse, all that is necessary is for the poet to indicate that they should be read so. If you aren't willing to submit to the poet's judgment, you needn't look or listen. There is no need to explain your unwillingness by trying to show a relationship between divisions of writing into verse-lines and the kind of language that the poet is using.

By printing poems by Simic and Haines as prose, Hayden Carruth wants to show that their line-divisions are not necessary, not shaped by a movement of language. But movement of language, which is sentence-structure, does not determine the structure of lines of verse. "Complacent suggestiveness, passiveness, inertness" of language—Carruth's description—are criticisms of the use of language, and therefore of tone, and ultimately of ideas. They are irrelevant, however, to the arranging of writing as lines of verse. When we are dealing with free verse, the lines are divided as they are because the poet wishes to divide them. It is a matter of impulse, not necessity.

I imagine that Carruth doesn't like the impulses of Haines and Simic. He doesn't like the tone of their writing, their attitudes, and their ideas. A great deal of what passes for analytic criticism is an attempt to explain, in an acceptable manner, what really can't be explained. The critic would not like the work in any case. If the poet used different language, and his line-divisions looked different, the critic still wouldn't like the poem. But to say so would be too personal, it wouldn't convince anyone, it wouldn't sound like criticism. So the critic attempts to show that the poet is really writing prose, because when you take away the divisions that he has put there, for the eye and the ear, the lines are no longer visible or audible.

Sandra McPherson

Heather bells. I suppose Hayden Carruth's piece did some good, after all, for it inspired her to say that she likes certain poems. The message of her writing is: I like this . . . and this . . . and this. But as far as reasoning goes: to say that, "We write in lines because we plant a vegetable garden in rows, because we have ribs, because. . ." It could just as well be said that we shouldn't write in lines because grass doesn't grow in lines, nor do forests, and water has many shapes.

The line is a unit of rhythm. The poet is moved by impulses of rhythm which he expresses in lines of verse. Impulse determines where each line breaks, and the impulse of the poem as a whole determines the look of the poem on the page or its sound in the air.

Images

The discussion of images that began in American poetry around 1910 may be a reflection of twentieth-century man's inability to make general statements in the face of a world that is increasingly unsure. We don't know what to believe, so we make an image.

Which is a sin, according to Scripture: "You shall not make graven images."

But the image according to Pound isn't graven—it is "that which presents an intellectual and emotional complex in an instant of time." Also, "One is trying to record the precise instant when a thing outward and objective transforms itself, or darts into a thing inward and subjective."

The image of the Imagists is a moment of perception, a movement of some sort. It is not just a sensation, a thing perceived by the senses. "Images in verse," said Hulme, "are not mere decoration, but the very essence of an intuitive language."

How does it work? The image as we have it from the Imagists and, ten years later, the Surrealists, is composed by bringing two entities together. Or three, or a dozen. The mind flies from one to the other.

In metaphor we are made to see the similarity between one thing and another: "My love is like a red, red rose." Metaphor suggests that things are really the same.

The image of the Imagists also brings different things together, but it doesn't merge them. Instead, a third thing is

This essay first appeared in *Field*, no. 23 (Fall 1980).

created . . . something unexpected. In Pound's famous poem about faces in a Metro station, the third thing is a black bough with petals. The faces of the people in the station have vanished, the station has vanished, to be replaced by a wet, black bough.

Surrealism uses the same technique, with this difference. The third thing is not like anything that we have seen or heard—it is not in nature, but purely invented.

> The sphere, colored orange, floating in space
> has a face with fixed brown eyes.
> Below the sphere a shirt with a tie
> in a dark, formal suit
> stands facing you, close to the parapet
> on the edge of the canyon.[1]

Moreover, the aim of Surrealism is to surprise, and the further apart things are, the more astonishing the effect when you juxtapose them. André Breton said, "To compare two subjects as distant as possible one from the other, or, by any other method, to bring them face to face, remains the highest task to which poetry can aspire."

Bringing together objects that appear to have nothing in common . . . this is the main Surrealist technique. It can be used mechanically, like every other poetic device, until it has lost its power to surprise. In the hands of a gifted poet, however, the technique can still produce the "intuition" of which Hulme spoke, Pound's "intellectual and emotional complex in an instant of time."

Juxtaposition of far-removed entities compels us to recognize that the mind is capable of anything and is its own master. "Man is the creator of values, which have their sense only from him and relative to him."[2]

But here we are confronted with a difficulty. If the mind is absolute master, aren't all images equally good? All poets equally interesting? But anyone who reads Surrealist poems, or poetry of any kind, soon realizes that some poets are more interesting than others: their images arouse more feeling, yield more pleasure, a keener surprise.

The painter Magritte said, "There exists a secret affinity between certain images; it holds equally for the objects represented by these images." I would put it another way: There is a secret affinity between objects, and if you perceive it your images will be alive.

But doesn't this talk of affinities bring us back to metaphor, a way of showing a likeness between things? Yes, the aim in creating metaphors or creating Symbolist, Imagist, or Surrealist images is the same: to show a meaning behind the veil of appearances. What difference is there between Baudelaire's forest, beloved of Symbolist poets, full of symbols that watch him with knowing eyes, and Breton's "facts which . . . present all the appearances of a signal"? In each case the poet is the receiver of signals from Beyond.

The images, however, are different. The image of the Symbolist, taken from the world perceived by the senses, is composed so as to evoke a trancelike state in the reader. The Symbolist image takes you away from the world, to the Over-Soul. The Symbolist poet would evade the world entirely, if he could.

The Imagist poet on the other hand believes with Hulme in a clear separation of earth and heaven. The image is a quick opening into another order of reality. Then it closes again. But, again, the principle is to show you something. Not just the sea and the pines . . . it is to be an "intuition."

The Surrealists went one better. The image would be entirely original, like nothing ever seen on earth. Again, however, the aim was the same: to reveal "a kind of absolute reality."

Whether we are speaking of Symbolist, Imagist, or Surrealist poets, it is their perception of affinities that is important. This is why some poets' images are alive. The poet has seen something happening between objects. Or the movement may be between ideas, as in Pound's *Cantos*.

In Williams's and Olson's theory of the poem as "a field of action," the poet himself is seen as an object in the field, interacting with other objects. I don't see why human beings have to be thought of as objects . . . I would think it fairly obvious that they aren't . . . but, in any case, in field theory also you are perceiving affinities. This is what the field looks like: juxtaposition of objects and a movement between them. A significance.

The poet's ability to see and feel affinities counts for much—some would say, for everything. In the hands of a poet such as Wordsworth, writing about the "spots of time," or Pound in some of the *Cantos,* images may evoke the supernatural.

> ... juxtaposition will be used to show metamorphosis, the changing of one thing into another, the breaking of solid surfaces that allows a permanent idea or god to emerge. ("A god is an eternal state of mind.") ... Pound's image, composed of parts in an active relationship, allows the supernatural to be seen. The image is an opening, "a 'magic moment' or moment of metamorphosis, bust thru from quotidien into 'divine' or 'permanent world.' Gods, etc." The eyes of a sea beast become the eyes of a girl, and these are the eyes of Helen, "destroyer of men and cities."[3]

American poets are still walking in the paths trodden by the Symbolists, Imagists, and Surrealists. They have found new names ... the "deep image," for example, to describe images with a certain psychological resonance or dreamlike quality. But only the name is new ... "deep images" were created by poets writing many years ago.

NOTES

1. Louis Simpson, "Magritte Shaving." *Caviare at the Funeral* (New York: Franklin Watts, 1980), 39.

2. Ferdinand Alquié, *The Philosophy of Surrealism* (Ann Arbor: University of Michigan Press, 1969), 102.

3. Louis Simpson, *Three on the Tower* (New York: William Morrow and Company, 1975), 35.

L'Ecriture Est-Elle Récuperable?

"L'écriture" veut dire "façon de dire." C'est ainsi qu'on a dépeint l'écriture dans le programme. Aussi, l'écriture doit "trouver en elle-même sa réussite, dans la conformité aux lois internes de son organisme vivant . . . la force de résister aux idéologies." Ainsi, il s'agit de l'écriture dans le sens ancien: l'art. Et on veut savoir si l'art peut survivre.

Pendant les ans récents on a vu des attaques: quelques-uns ont dit que l'écriture va disparaître; l'avenir appartient aux appareils électroniques. Les gouvernements se sont servis de l'écriture sans admettre qu'elle possède des lois internes. Mais il n'y a pas besoin de chercher des exemples effrayants de la pression politique pour voir que l'écriture—voulant dire la poésie, le roman, et le drame écrit—soit en danger. Il ne faut que regarder la vie normale en tout pays—aux Etats-Unis ou dans la Russie. La plupart des gens ne lisent pas les romans bien écrits. Quant à la poésie, pour la plupart des gens c'est une chose absolument inconnue ou mal comprise.

Assurément, l'écriture n'est pas récupérable si l'écriture dépend du public. Et l'avenir ne sera pas meilleur pour l'écri-

---

This talk was given at a symposium in Montreal, October 5–8, 1974. The subject of discussion may be translated: "Can Writing Be Recovered?" The meaning of this did not seem clear to the participants, and the discussion ranged from French-Canadian nationalism to the most recent poststructuralist ideas brought piping hot from Paris. My own remarks were to the effect that I didn't know if writing could be recovered but I wrote because I had to anyway.

The talk was reprinted in *liberté* 17, nos. 97–98 (Montreal, January–April 1975).

vain qui dépend du public. Mais cette pensée ne me fait pas avoir peur. Quand j'ai commencé à écrire je ne pensais pas que personne voudrait lire ce que j'écrivais. Il s'est fait que des poèmes que j'ai écrits furent publiés. Mais je n'ai pas changé mes habitudes pour cette raison. J'ai écrit pendant trente ans pour le plaisir d'écrire. Je ne pense pas au public, mais à ce que je veux dire et la façon de dire.

Il n'y a personne qui sait ce qui va arriver dans le monde. Mais nous pouvons décider ce que nous allons faire nous-mêmes. L'homme aussi a des lois internes. Quand je trouve que j'ai quatre ou cinq heures devant moi, sans interruptions—quand je peux écrire, je suis parfaitement content. Si le monde veut se passer de l'écriture cela sera triste, mais moi je ne sais pas m'en passer.

Je sais bien que ce que j'ai dit rappelle la tour d'ivoire. Je sais ce qu'on peut dire touchant la responsabilité de l'écrivain. En effet, l'écrivain est un homme comme les autres; peut-être il est père de famille. Il peut avoir une croyance religieuse ou politique. Je ne tente pas de nier que l'écrivain peut être conscient de la vie de son temps, même actif. Mais, à mesure qu'il est écrivain il doit travailler á crèer une réalité qui ne dépend pas de l'opinion publique. L'écriture est un organisme vivant, ce n'est pas un commentaire.

Et si le monde ne veut pas attendre les écritures? La pensée indépendante, que vaut-elle? A ce moment, les jeunes surtout trouvent incompréhensible l'idéal de l'auteur dans son cabinet, filant une toile. La vie d'un Flaubert, d'un Proust, la vie d'un Joyce qui devient aveugle en travaillant—quel égotisme! Pour se faire appeler grand homme . . . C'est la vue de bien des jeunes. La vie d'auteur appartient au dix-neuvième siècle, quand les grands égoïstes étaient en vogue. Et du reste, l'originalité est un concept économique. Le mot "grand" vend les livres. Au fond, l'originalité est capitaliste.

Maints jeunes souscrivent à ce point de vue—et je ne parle pas des jeunes ignorants, mais un nombre assez grand des plus intelligents. Je pense que cette vue pose un danger grave pour l'écriture—plus grave que les attaques par les gouvernements ou les groupes politiques. Il y a dedans une vérité que je ne sais pas, et de plus, je ne voudrais pas, contredire, parce que, en grand mésure, je suis du même avis. Je n'aime pas le spéctacle des écrivains égoïstes. Je n'aime pas "son et lumière." Bien que j'ai toujours pensé que l'originalité ait été la qualité suprême de l'art, je peux voir que l'originalité peut être sans valeur. Si on regarde l'histoire de la peinture—plutôt l'histoire des galeries, on peut voir que l'originalité est souvent une proposition commerciale. Et l'indépendance peut être une solitude. Les cathédrales ne sont pas construites par des hommes solitaires; les oeuvres dramatiques non plus. Quant à la poésie, à ce moment aux Etats-Unis—je parle de mon pays parce que je le connais mieux que les autres pays, et de la poésie parce que j'écris des poèmes—aux Etats-Unis la poésie se limite à deux modes: une poésie confessionnelle, c'est-à-dire, qui révèle la vie de l'auteur, et une poésie imagiste qui tente d'être mystique. La poésie aux Etats-Unis manque la narration et le drame. C'est parce que les poètes ne croient pas qu'ils ont quelque chose à dire touchant la société. Dans leurs poèmes on ne trouve pas les sentiments qu'ont les gens, l'un pour l'autre.

A résumer. D'une part je crois que pour la plupart des gens l'écriture n'est pas une chose nécessaire. Je crois que cette situation va continuer. D'autre part je crois que l'écriture est une façon de vivre—il y a des personnes qui doivent écrire. Je suis content que les choses soient ainsi. Je peux imaginer ce que je devrais écrire pour attirer le public. Ça ne serait pas l'écriture—du moins, je n'aurais pas plaisir à écrire ces choses.

Je ne suis pas le renard dans la fable. Si je parle comme le renard, c'est parce que j'ai goûté à ces raisins, et c'est vrai, ils étaient verts. Je suis reconnaissant des assistances petites, et je vous conseille d'en faire autant.

Poetry in a Cold Climate

A mere handful of poets have an audience, and in each case there are special circumstances—the poet has written a best-selling novel or has a message to deliver. But the poet who has no message and no novel is out in the cold. Talk to such a one and you may be told that his book, in spite of good reviews, sold only three thousand copies before being remaindered. And this in a nation of . . . what was it yesterday? Two hundred and thirty million. It appears that one American in seventy-six thousand will buy a book of poetry for the hell of it.

Don't blame the publishers—they are eager to provide any kind of writing that will turn a profit: diet books, "romance" novels, the reminiscences of burglars and call girls. Don't blame the bookstores—think of the overhead! They can't afford to give poetry shelf space, unless it's by Rod McKuen. For every copy of Robert Frost's poetry that moves—not to mention yours and mine—they can dispose of hundreds of *The Passion and the Rage* by Elizabeth Godwin ("Theirs was a love scorched by treason and dangerous destiny"), or *Sweet Abandon* by Wendy Lozano ("He turned her vows of purity into the fires of love!").

This is a revised version of a talk I gave at the State University of New York at Stony Brook on March 1, 1983, and again at Trinity College, Hartford, Connecticut, on March 8. The poems "Encounter on the 7:07," "In a Time of Peace," and "The Unwritten Poem" were published in *The Best Hour of the Night* (New York: Ticknor and Fields, 1983). Copyright © 1983 by Louis Simpson. Reprinted by permission of Ticknor and Fields, a Houghton Mifflin Company.

Let's face it . . . the public doesn't feel the slightest need for poetry as it goes about its daily round of getting and spending.

"What is a Poet?" said Wordsworth. "To whom does he address himself? And what language is to be expected from him?" Wordsworth answered his own question: "The poet is a man speaking to men: a man, it is true, endowed with more lively sensibility, more enthusiasm and tenderness, who has a greater knowledge of human nature, and a more comprehensive soul, than are supposed to be common among mankind." But—these are not Wordsworth's words but mine—it appears that, perhaps alone among nations, the people of the United States do not think that the poet has a greater knowledge of human nature and a more comprehensive soul.

I once traveled to a poetry festival in Macedonia. Poets had been invited by the government to stay at a hotel on Lake Ohrid, to give readings of their poetry and take part in panel discussions, and to travel to other towns and villages where they would give readings. The poets came from several countries of Western and Eastern Europe—from Italy, France, the United Kingdom, Denmark, and Norway; from Hungary, Roumania, East Germany, and the Soviet Union. There was also a contingent of four poets from the United States. On our arrival at the airport we were met by the Macedonian poet who had made the arrangements, and driven to the hotel. There each of us was given a sheaf of printed material that described the festival, and a certain amount of Macedonian currency to make our stay more pleasant.

On the first evening the poets held a reading in the open air. A crowd of people from the surrounding area put on their best suits and dresses and came to hear the foreign poets. The poems were read with translations and the audience applauded vigorously.

The next day we met again in a large auditorium. At every seat there were earphones through which one could hear the speakers being translated into several languages. There were panel discussions during the day, and in the evening there would be poetry readings. In the lobby outside the auditorium the books of the participating poets were on display—with one exception: there were no books by the American poets. The American embassy had not undertaken to provide any, and in fact would not have been able to. The American ambassador had been invited to attend, but had sent his wife instead. She had never heard the names of the American poets, and seemed surprised by the idea of a poetry festival. Were there people in the world who actually took poetry seriously? Apparently there were, for every day while the festival lasted the auditorium was packed, and the readings and discussions were reported in the newspapers and on television and over the radio. What the American poets had to say was avidly reported. The ambassador's wife must have felt like Alice in Wonderland, surrounded by bizarre creatures speaking phrases and sentences that made no sense, yet who seemed to understand one another.

Our government, I think, may be unique in its ignorance of the esteem in which poets are held throughout the world. A Russian poet once told me, "In Russia poets are like your senators. Two or three poets get together for an evening, and the next day what they said is talked about all over Moscow." In the USSR poetry is news, and maybe the only real news they get. Copies of poems are circulated from hand to hand. When poets criticize the government they may be arrested and charged with "parasitism," and sent to do hard labor, or confined in a mental hospital. No doubt about it, life can be made unpleasant for a poet in Russia. In the United States, on the other hand, nothing a poet thinks or says appears to make the slightest difference.

So I am inclined to think. Yet in the 1960s poets did make a difference—they were among the first to protest against our involvement in Vietnam; their words reached hundreds and thousands of young people who then went out and opposed the war, so that at last there was a movement for peace that could not be ignored. The protesters may not have stopped the war, but they made it difficult, and finally impossible, for the Administration to claim that it had a mandate to engage in a full-scale war in Asia.

The poets made a difference—but not the poetry. Insofar as the speeches poets made from platforms, or the poems they read aloud, reflected the views of the peace-marchers, poets were welcome. But if they read poems that had no political message they were shuffled off the platform. The Left has no more love of poetry than the Right.

The antipathy of our citizens for poetry goes back to the beginnings of the nation. The first American colonists, the Puritans, had a religious aversion for poetry which they associated with the profligacy of courts. As the country developed there was a pressing need for men who could use an axe or plough, a need for blacksmiths and shipbuilders, a need for shopkeepers, but there was never a need for those who, as Yeats says, "articulate sweet sounds together." In the New World poets, who had been honored in the Old, would be regarded with contempt, and so they have been regarded ever since, for the character given to a nation at the start is the mould for succeeding generations. In the United States poets have always been regarded as extraneous. The so-called performing arts have become respectable, and novelists and other writers of prose have won respect by the money they make. But poets do not make as much as street-cleaners. To Wordsworth's claim that poets have a greater knowledge of human nature than the common man, the common man replies by tapping his temple with his finger. Poets must be crazy.

But when did the common man read poetry? Not in Renaissance Italy, nor England under the Tudors, nor in the France of Louis XIV. A taste for poetry was restricted to the aristocracy. In the eighteenth century, with the rise of the middle class, education became popular, and those who could read were accustomed to reading verse. The educated man or woman would have read Pope's "Rape of the Lock" or Goldsmith's "Deserted Village" and have an opinion on the subject. But in our century education has ceased to include the understanding of poetry. Most of those who have had what is called a higher education know nothing about poetry. Classes in literature are taught at the university, but our future engineers, lawyers, doctors, heads of corporations, and heads of government do not attend them. The leaders of the nation know no poetry at all.

I can imagine what the engineer or head of government would say to this. Poetry, he would say, is nonsense—why should we read it? There are more urgent matters to be attended to, a hundred pressing questions of economy, and affairs of state.

"Where there is no vision," Scripture tells us, "the people perish." If poetry doesn't make sense, what shall we say of business and government when they are conducted by men and women who have no poetry? Are their policies making sense? It is not a figure of speech to say that many are perishing in our country. The twelve million unemployed must feel that they are perishing.

If I were giving advice to a poet I would say, "Poetry will never be popular—you must learn to do your work regardless of praise or blame. In any case, as a poet has said, "No art ever yet grew by looking into the eyes of the public."

Your task is to tell the truth—for truth's sake and the pleasure it gives. For there is delight in saying a thing exactly.

Do not fall into an error which will make your writing small and unimportant—that is, to think that because the public has no interest in poetry, the poet need not concern himself with public matters, but address his writing to a coterie, or that he may speak disjointedly and confusedly because no one is listening.

Write as though you were writing for millions, though only ten should hear. It was so that Milton and Wordsworth and our own Whitman wrote. Do you think that their books were read by the crowd? They were read by only a few, but these carried the word. The poets did not say to themselves, "As only aesthetes read my poems I shall write only precious things, in riddles that only the initiate may understand." On the contrary, they wrote about the life of the nation, in a language, as Wordsworth recommends, of a man speaking to men. I would advise you to do the same. Do not mind that your books are not read—if you write about real things, one day they will be.

The life around you is not poetic—in fact, seems to repel poetry. But if it were aesthetically attractive, if instead of a shopping mall there stood a Taj Mahal, what need would there be for your writing? Your poems would be merely decorative. Instead, the life you see around you, the asphalt roads, and the litter along the roads, offers you countless opportunities. Instead of resenting the banality of it all you should be grateful. This everyday world cries out for poetry.

I live in an area of shopping centers and housing developments, much the same as you would find on the outskirts of Iowa City or Los Angeles—a fair testing-ground of the American average. I have frequently doubted that it is possible to make poetry out of circumstances that are so banal. And if I did write poetry, who would read it? Certainly not the people who live across the street.

But I have come to realize what poets have always said. Coleridge wrote:

> I may not hope from outward forms to win
> The passion and the life, whose fountains are within.

When your feelings and imagination are exhausted this is a hard saying. On the other hand it could encourage you to search for poetry in yourself. Then you may find it more rewarding to live in a house on Long Island than a villa in Italy. The villa is finished; the terraces, the formal gardens, the cypresses, and olive groves, were planted in an arrangement long ago. The people in the village have their settled ways, going back for centuries. They don't want to change, and don't need your poems. But nothing is yet settled where you live—everything is still to be done.

I have spoken of one error. There is another, related to the first. It is easy to satirize the kind of life we have: the mania for owning things, our fads, the lies of politicians, and so on. Satire is a tame kind of revenge, and a number of poets have written satirically about our culture—it is the easiest target in the world, with the exception of the culture of the Soviet

Union. But though these television-watching, floor-waxing, detergent-comparing lives seem to lack intelligence and a sense of purpose, if this is all you see you haven't gone to the root of the matter. Satire describes surfaces and aims to be amusing at the expense of the subject. Poetry, on the other hand, submits to truth, though it may be less entertaining or cause the reader to feel uncomfortable.

The instrument that measures is part of the experiment and affects the result. The poet is involved with the thing he is describing. This is why poetry has qualities of sympathy and understanding. And this is why it is difficult to be a poet: one must have paid with one's feelings for every statement one makes about the world. It is the sense of the poet's having experienced the things he is writing about that gives the poet's writing its authority.

I am not saying that the poet must be just like the people he lives among, or share their attitudes—of course not, for to write one must be able to see the subject, and this means standing away from it. The poet, as Whitman said, is "both in and out of the game."

The best advice, however, is not as good as setting an example, and I shall read three poems in which I have attempted to realize my ideas. In the first, "Encounter on the 7:07," I seem to be taking issue with Wordsworth. You may have noticed that I have cited Wordsworth more than once—this is because he is one of the few writers on the subject of poetry who says anything important, and what he had to say in 1800 seems even more urgent today. I seem to be disagreeing with his remarks about nature, to be saying that a love of nature is no longer necessary to our well-being. But as the poem proceeds you will see that I am not disagreeing with Wordsworth—I am saying that circumstances have changed and that we must adapt his ideas to new circumstances.

Encounter on the 7:07

He got on at Cold Spring Harbor
and took the seat next to mine—
a man of about forty, with a suntan.

The doctor said, "You need a vacation."
His wife said, "It's an opportunity,
we can visit my sister in Florida."

He played golf every day
and they visited the Everglades.
Trees standing out of the swamp
with moss and vines hanging down,
ripples moving through the water . . .

An alligator is different from a crocodile,
it has a broad head, et cetera.

*

There's a car card advertising
"Virginia Slims"—a photographer's model
got up to look like a cowgirl
in boots and a ten-gallon hat.
She's kneeling with a cigarette in her hand
and a smile—in spite of the warning
printed below: "The Surgeon General
has determined that cigarette smoking
is dangerous to your health."

It's the American way
not to be daunted—to smoke cigarettes
and rope cattle all you want.

The man sitting next to me,
whose name is Jerry—Jerry DiBello—
observes that he doesn't smoke cigarettes,
he smokes cigars. "Look at Winston Churchill.
He smoked cigars every day of his life,
and he lived to be over eighty."

*

Wordsworth said that the passions
of people who live in the country
are incorporated with the beautiful
and permanent forms of nature.
In the suburbs they are incorporated
with the things you see from the train:
rows of windshields . . . a factory . . .

a housing development, all the houses
alike, either oblong or square,
like the houses and hotels in a game of *Monopoly.*

A crane, bright orange, bearing the name "Slattery" . . .

"Feldman," a sign says, "Lumber."
A few miles further on . . .
"Feldman, Wood Products."

*

"The Old Coachman Bar and Grill" . . .

His family used to own a restaurant
on 25A . . . DiBello's.

His father came from Genoa
as a seaman, and jumped ship.
In the middle of the night
he went up on deck,
put his shoes and clothes in a bag,
hung it around his neck,
stood on the rail, and jumped.

He swam to shore and hid in the bushes.
The next day he started walking . . .
came to a restaurant and asked for a job
washing dishes. Ten years later
he owned the restaurant.

Jerry didn't go into the business.
He sells automobiles,
has his own Buick-Pontiac showroom.
It's hard to make a living these days.
The government ought to clamp down on the Japanese
flooding the market with their Datsuns.

But I'm not listening—I'm on deck,
looking at the lights of the harbor.
A sea wind fans my cheek.
I hear the waves chuckling
against the side of the ship.

I grasp the iron stanchion,
climb onto the rail,

take a deep breath,
and jump.

*

I've brought along *Ulysses*
and am just passing the time of day
with old Troy of the D.M.P.
when be damned but a bloody sweep comes along
and near drives his gear in my eye.

"An *olla putrida* . . .
old fags and cabbage-stumps of quotations,"
said Lawrence. Drawing a circle about himself
and Frieda . . . building an ark,
envisioning the Flood.

But the Flood may be long coming.
In the meantime there is life
every day, and Ennui.

Ever since the middle class
and money have ruled our world
we have been desolate.

                              Like Emma Bovary
in the beech-copse, watching her dog
yapping about, chasing a butterfly.

A feeling of being alone
and separate from the world . . .
"alienation" psychiatrists call it.
Religion would say, this turning away
from life is the life of the soul.

This is why Joyce is such a great writer:
he shows a life of fried bread
and dripping "like a boghole,"
and art that rises out of life
and flies toward the sun,

transfiguring as it flies
the reality . . . Joe Hynes,
Alf Bergan, Bob Doran,

and the saint of the quotidian
himself, Leopold Bloom.

*

Jerry has a gang who meet every Saturday
to play poker. For friendly stakes . . .
you can lose twenty or thirty dollars,
that's all. It's the camaraderie
that counts.

           They talk about the ball game,
politics, tell the latest jokes . . .

One of the guys sells insurance,
another works at the firehouse.

As if reading my mind . . .
"Don't take us for a bunch of bobos."
There's a chemist who works for Westinghouse,
and a lawyer who's on permanent retainer
with the Long Island Lighting Company.

What, he asks, do I do?

I tell him, and he says, it figures.
The way I was so lost in a book
he could see that I live in a different world.

*

In Florida after the storm
the whole area for miles inland
was littered with trees and telephone poles,
wrecked automobiles, houses that had blown down.
There was furniture, chairs and sofas,
lying in the street, buried in mud.

For days afterwards they were still finding bodies.

When he went for a walk
the shore looked as though it had been swept
with a broom. The sky was clear,
the sun was shining, and the sea was calm.

He felt that he was alone with the universe.
He, Jerry DiBello, was at one with God.

The second poem, "In a Time of Peace," addresses itself to matters that could be targets of satire—tourism, the quest for distraction, the need to buy things. But you will see that the treatment is not satiric—not, at any rate, in the conclusion.

In a Time of Peace

He changes dollars into francs
and walks, from Rue de Rivoli
almost to the Arc de Triomphe.

He sits at a sidewalk café
and looks at the ones who are passing.
Then goes to a restaurant
and a show.

        Someone told him the Crazy Horse
is the place to go, "un spectacle de deux heures"
you can understand "if you're Javanese,
dead drunk, or mentally retarded."
There are sketches, stripteases:
blonde Solange, black Marianne,
Ingrid with her boots and whip . . .
and who can forget Duzia,
"the most wanted girl in Europe"?

The chorus in the entr'actes
jump and squeal. Imagining
their own nudity is driving them mad.

After the show he chooses to walk.
The lamps in leafy avenues
shining on monuments and statues . . .

             *

A sea of amethyst is breaking
along two miles of beach umbrellas . . .
the car parks, red roofs
of the bathing establishments,
Lidino, Antaura . . . advertisements
for Stock, Coca-Cola,
"tutte le Sera DISCOTECA."

A child on the crowded sand
is playing with a new toy.
It hurls an object into the air,
a parachute opens, and descends . . .
homunculus, a little plastic man
returning from Outer Space.

Some day we may have to live there,
but for the present life consists
of sex . . . all the beautiful bodies
that you see on the beach;
food—there are dozens of places,
ranging from the ice cream parlor
to Tito's—Ristorante Tito del Molo;
things to buy: Galletti for handbags,
Timpano for a lighter;
and entertainment: the Cinema Odeon,
the bar with pinball machines.
There is even a Sauna Finlandese.

At night the promenade glitters,
loud music fills the air.
Not good music . . . but it doesn't matter
to the families with small children
or to the lovers.

Finally, "The Unwritten Poem." Last summer I traveled to Italy at the expense of a foundation. I was given a suite of rooms overlooking Lake Como and looking across at the Alps, and was expected to write. Perfect circumstances, some would say, but in a month I wrote nothing. Three months after I had returned to my own place with its views of some trees, a wire fence, and a rusting iron table, I wrote "The Unwritten Poem."

The Unwritten Poem

You will never write the poem about Italy.
What Socrates said about love
is true of poetry—where is it?
Not in beautiful faces and distant scenery
but the one who writes and loves.

In your life here, on this street
where the houses from the outside
are all alike, and so are the people.
Inside, the furniture is dreadful—
floc on the walls, and huge color television.

To love and write unrequited
is the poet's fate. Here you'll need
all your ardor and ingenuity.
This is the front and these are the heroes—
a life beginning with "Hi!" and ending with "So long!"

You must rise to the sound of the alarm
and march to catch the 6:20—
watch as they ascend the station platform
and, grasping briefcases, pass beyond your gaze
and hurl themselves into the flames.

UNDER DISCUSSION
Donald Hall, General Editor

Volumes in the Under Discussion series collect reviews and essays about individual poets. The series is concerned with contemporary American and English poets about whom the consensus has not yet been formed and the final vote has not been taken. Titles in the series include:

Elizabeth Bishop and Her Art
  edited by Lloyd Schwartz and Sybil P. Estess
Richard Wilbur's Creation *edited and with an*
  Introduction by Wendy Salinger
Reading Adrienne Rich
  edited by Jane Roberta Cooper
On the Poetry of Allen Ginsberg
  edited by Lewis Hyde
Robert Bly: When Sleepers Awake
  edited by Joyce Peseroff

Forthcoming volumes will examine the work of Robert Creeley, H.D., Galway Kinnell, and Louis Simpson, among others.

Please write for further information on available editions and current prices.

Ann Arbor   **The University of Michigan Press**